Let's Stop Calling It an Achievement Gap

A Volume in Research in
Contemporary Perspectives on Access, Equity and Achievement

Series Editor

Chance Lewis
University of North Carolina at Charlotte

Contemporary Perspectives on Access, Equity, and Achievement

Chance W. Lewis, Editor

(List continues on next page)

Let's Stop Calling It an Achievement Gap

by

Autumn A. Arnett

INFORMATION AGE PUBLISHING, INC.
Charlotte, NC • www.infoagepub.com

Library of Congress Cataloging-in-Publication Data

CIP record for this book is available from the Library of Congress
http://www.loc.gov

ISBNs: 978-1-64113-518-4 (Paperback)

         978-1-64113-519-1 (Hardcover)

         978-1-64113-520-7 (ebook)

CONTENTS

ACKNOWLEDGMENTS

I would like to extend my thanks to the following individuals:

To the series editor, Dr. Chance Lewis, who provided the initial prodding to "write the book," and who afforded complete autonomy to shape the finished product while offering guidance and support throughout the process.

To my family, who supported me during the extensive travel required to conduct the investigations, and in particular my mom, Tonya, who filled in on multiple occasions to assume the daily responsibilities of caring for my children while I was away.

To my pastor, John A. Cherry II, whose mention of the achievement gap and relentless emphasis on breaking the associated stereotypes resonated with me as a child and sparked in me a lifelong interest in the disparate educational outcomes for black children in this country.

To all of the individuals who agreed to sit for interviews and write chapter introductions to shape the narratives on the page that follow. In addition to those whose names appear in the following chapters, I'd like to thank Eric Baylor, Thomas Butler, George French, Shan Williams, Jr., and Latraniecesa Wilson for their assistance with securing interviews and providing feedback along the way.

Let's Stop Calling It an Achievement Gap, pp. xi–xi

INTRODUCTION

The exclusion of Black students from the public education system in this country predates the formation of the United States as a sovereign nation.

On February 13, 1635, Boston Latin School opened as America's first public school. Blacks were specifically and intentionally barred from attending, even though there were a number of free Blacks living in the region at the time. (Massachusetts was also a big slave-holding state, and a major center of the slave trade in the 17th and 18th century, but even the free Black students could not attend the "public" school.)

When we talk about returning the power of education back to states and eliminating the federal Department of Education, we have to first examine the record of individual states in educating Black children throughout the years. Between 1980 and 2005, 45 states were involved in lawsuits around equity of funding and adequacy of education provided to all students in the state (West & Peterson, 2006). However, when the courts "tried to legislate the particulars of racial balance within jurisdictional boundaries, they entered into a political morass from which they could not easily extricate themselves without doing harm to their own prestige or to the very principle that they had set forth" (West & Peterson, 2006). Due to the separation of powers in states, it was not enough for the courts to rule these inequities existed; legislators still had no motivation or desire to correct them.

Today, many of the states recognized as having the best public education system also have the greatest inequities, caused not by inferiority or an

Let's Stop Calling It an Achievement Gap, pp. xiii–xvi
Copyright © 2019 by Information Age Publishing

inability of certain students to learn, but by persistently unequally funded and underresourced schools which have maintained a de facto separate and unequal system of public education for students within the state.

And while even the federal government has not done enough to ensure appropriate access to quality education for all of these groups, it has to be the role of the federal government to set and enforce an educational standard around access for every student in the country.

In a recent conversation, former House Education Committee Chair George Miller said, it is the Constitutional responsibility of the federal government to "provide a first-class education to every child and young person … in the country," a responsibility which many states, even the country as a whole, have failed to uphold. Miller pointed out that over the years, many states "weren't meeting that constitutional obligation to poor and minority students and students with disabilities," an issue No Child Left Behind initially sought out to remedy, he said.

When you get to higher education, the disparities are even worse. A recent report from The Education Trust (Del Pilar, Nichols, & Schak, 2018) found there has been no movement on closing the degree attainment gap between Blacks and Whites in this country in 20 years. The persistent underfunding of neighborhood schools continues through to persistent underfunding of historically Black colleges and universities, which were only established because Black students after Reconstruction, both newly-freed and never-bound, were not permitted to attend the existing institutions of learning in this country.

Community colleges and regional institutions, which also serve a higher number of Black students, are also under funded. A 2018 study from the Center for American Progress found public 2- and 4-year institutions spend more than $1,000 less on Black and Latino students than their White counterparts (Garcia, 2018).

During all of the ire around Betsy DeVos' confirmation as U.S. Secretary of Education, one heated Twitter exchange appeared in which one Black woman expressed concern for the future of education of her children, while a White, gay man expressed a different viewpoint, but said he is also part of a vulnerable population. But there is no more vulnerable position than that of a Black/brown child/family in a country which is built on the exclusion of Black and brown people. While other races have been oppressed throughout the history of this country, they have found acceptance and relief by joining in the hatred and oppression of Black people, leaving only those with darker skin hues at the bottom of the totem pole of vulnerability.

When we talk about an academic achievement gap in this country, we must do so in the context of an opportunity gap, which has said to Black and brown children that they are not worthy of accessing the same quality of education as their white peers. We must talk about it in the context of implicit and explicit biases held by educators, assessment companies and legislators, which continue to box these children out, even after the courts said you must let them in. We must talk about it in the context of all of the teacher turnover and instability in their schools, because of the high pressure environments facing the teachers who are forced to work with too few resources, and, yes, the high numbers of unprepared or uncommitted doers-good who go to teach children in predominantly Black schools without any ability to identify with those students' lives. We must talk about it in the context of intentional federal policy which has failed our most vulnerable students.

The academic achievement gap is an adult problem; it's less a reflection of the students it measures than an indictment on the failure of the adults entrusted with providing a quality education for all students in this country.

REFERENCES

Del Pilar, W., Nichols, A., & Schak, J. O. (2018, June 14). *The state of higher education equity*. Retrieved from https://edtrust.org/the-state-of-higher-education-equity/

Garcia, S. (2018, April 5). *Gaps in college spending shortchange students of color*. Retrieved https://www.americanprogress.org/issues/education-postsecondary/reports/2018/04/05/448761/gaps-college-spending-shortchange-students-color/

West, M., & Peterson, P. (2006). The adequacy lawsuit: A critical appraisal. In *School money trials: The legal pursuit of educational adequacy*. Washington, DC: Brookings Institution Press.

CHAPTER 1

ATLANTA

INTRODUCTION

Born and raised in Atlanta in the 1970s, I attended Atlanta Public Schools at Walter F. White Elementary ('82), Sutton Middle School ('85), and Northside High School ('89). In elementary school, I was surrounded by educated, lower- to middle-class families in a predominantly Black neighborhood. It was a community that set the standards high on education, making sure that we had all that we needed no matter what anyone's circumstances were. We were a proud community who encouraged one another that you can become anything that you believe. We didn't realize at the time that there was a difference between the resources available to us compared to the schools across town.

I wasn't a student without a struggle. I was one of the students who wrestled with reading and writing, so I was assessed and placed with a support team, teacher and reading/literacy coach to get me up to speed in reading and assistance with my writing skills. Although there were efforts made to help me improve, there was still not enough time in the day, nor enough staff or resources available to give me the undivided attention I needed to narrow the gap and help me catch up with others in my grade level. It was an uphill battle for me all the way up until college.

In the early 80s, I was bused across town to the Buckhead area to attend Sutton Middle School with a diverse group of students, teachers and

Let's Stop Calling It an Achievement Gap, pp. 1–11
Copyright © 2019 by Information Age Publishing
All rights of reproduction in any form reserved.

administrators. It was here that I discovered a new world of opportunity, a new reality that whatever I needed was right at my disposal, but I didn't quite identify as a beneficiary. It was all new to me, an oasis of resources: the facilities, equipment, textbooks, space for all types of accommodations in drama, chorus, band and orchestra and we had both an upper and lower field to play and practice any sport we could imagine.

Often I wondered when I would travel to and from school, why were these schools different than the ones I had known as a younger child? What was it about our side of town that didn't allow those who were unable to attend the schools in the north to receive the same services and offerings? Maybe people on the North side were smarter, perhaps they were wealthier, maybe even better than us. I am sure I was not the only one to think about that from time to time. I am sure that there are others who still believe that they are not worthy to have the equal opportunities for education.

I would go on to attend Northside School of Performing Arts, where I was placed in an environment that was not limited to specific pathways of learning but introduced several potential roads of success. That's when I realized, Wow, there is more to life than my immediate neighborhood —what I read in books is right here in front of me. The place where I discovered my love for art, music, dance, and athletics, where I would letter in five sports (basketball, track, cross country, soccer, and cheerleading). I was even fortunate to travel my 11th-grade year to Italy with the tour show.

My experiences were very different than those of some of my peers in the neighborhood. As an adult, I've come to realize that all of those questions I grappled with as an adolescent about whether we were just as deserving or just as smart as the other students were incredibly damaging. Why is it that we keep calling attainment deficits between Black and White students an achievement gap, but not acknowledging the gap is all about our priorities? Why not provide the resources needed to get the job done, to narrow the gap, to move the needle? Every child deserves the best education. You can't improve or meet standards if you don't have the tools to achieve such a goal. It was when I received the tools I needed that I began to improve my skill set, my self-esteem, and change my perspective to believe that I am smart, capable and loved.

For me it is not about Black or White, socioeconomic background, wrong or right. It is about giving every child a chance to reach their highest potential. I have had the opportunity to work in partnership with Atlanta Public Schools, DeKalb and Fulton County School Systems. Each system continues to struggle with persistent achievement gaps, and each is working to find ways to increase attendance and graduation rates while serving the social-emotional needs of all students. However, the problem still exists, we are still not doing all we can and even when we try, we often fail to meet the mark.

In my current position, I am empowered to be a change agent in the educational system to provide the support needed to save children's lives and help them stay on the right track. I am an advocate for education, educators and supporting schools and the students and parents we serve. Students should not have to think about what we can do to make a difference in our schools, it occurs to me that students should not have to be placed on a waiting list to attend a good school or create the temptation for parents to falsify their residential information so that their children can attend a school that sets them up for success. Every school should be adequately resourced to provide a quality education for each of the students within its walls.

As we continue to tussle with why we can't have all the resources we need to improve the performance of our schools, it's important that we continue to find ways to leverage the strengths of the community for the benefit of the students. Whether it is clean clothes, help with school work or someone to talk to when things get tough, there are a number of nonacademic factors that can be improved by volunteers or mentors from business to help improve student success in the classroom.

As an educator who has worked in elementary, middle and high schools, as well as a technical college, two-year college and served as an adjunct professor and campus dean, I am fully convinced that a collaborative model is the way to go to help students at every level of their education.

Dr. Angela Williams, an Atlanta native, currently serves as site coordinator for Communities in Schools for Atlanta at Love T. Nolan Elementary School. She has worked as a K–12 educator, as well as a professor and administrator in various institutions of higher education.

ATLANTA

"A City Full of Colleges"
Its Students Can't Access

Before Atlanta became ground zero for one of the largest cheating scandals in the nation's history in 2013, Atlanta Public Schools was considered a model district. Then-Superintendent Beverly Hall was named superintendent of the year in 2009, even as the state Board of Education was uncovering evidence of cheating on tests in schools across the city.

According to Brian A. Williams, who serves as director of the Crim Center for Urban Education Excellence at Georgia State University, "The cheating scandal opened the door for conversations around school quality and accountability, so that's kind of the name of the game here. There's a lot of pressure from the top to make sure students are 'achieving.' There's lots of conversations about 'failing schools,' and that's very arbitrary."

Sometimes schools that are on an upward trajectory are still labeled as failing and closed, said Williams.

Some advocates say they saw the crisis coming when Hall was hired 10 years prior, though they did not know exactly what would happen.

Ed Johnson, an Atlanta businessman and education advocate, says Skinner-esque behaviorism practices and the concept of scientific management Hall brought into the district created an environment which was sure to lead to disaster, one in which bonuses were tied to test scores and actual content mastery took a back seat.

"You only need to look to businesses, which is where [these incentive practices are] predominantly applied, to see that it doesn't work," Johnson said. "People are put in position to conform, as opposed to being creative. But those practices destroy ... intrinsic motivation and substitutes extrinsic motivation, rewards and punishment. When you put an incentive out there, the objective becomes to get the incentive ... and they did it to such an extent that it became really systemic—system-wide. ... The objective was to get the incentive, not to improve teaching and learning."

But Johnson said the practices were primarily implemented in the predominantly Black schools south of I-20, which remain primarily attended by Black children. "The whole thing became very perverse," Johnson said. "When you bring that kind of practice into a school system, where you're dealing with young kids, especially young Black kids, and you impose that on them, you only make their problems worse, and you make the teachers who are inspiring them worse. You're not inspiring the teachers to be the best that they can be, especially for Black children exposed to a lot of poverty."

"What's really unfortunate," said Williams, "is that many of the decisions that are being made are being made by people of color." Though current superintendent Meria Joel Carstaphen has classroom experience, Williams said many of the school board actions are more in line with those who favor privatization.

"The people that are at the helm are Black and brown people. We do have a lot of people who are on our school board—and also people who are in charge of governance, in terms of our superintendent who have roots in" Teach for America and other charter school organizations, he said.

"There's This Thinking That Black Kids Need to be Trained"

There is concern by some that charter schools, many of which tout strict "no-excuses" discipline philosophies, perpetuate inequities in education, and suspend Black students at higher rates than their White counterparts. "It's the KIPP model—the very basic, rudimentary model to education that's very much about controlling every single thing that the student does, whether it's how they're sitting in their seat or how they're walking down the hall," said Williams. "Social control as a way of educating children— it's not about you being educated, it's about you being controlled. ... That's what education boils down to for poor Black and brown children."

Research shows that though charters typically enroll more Black students, they may suspend fewer (Barnum, 2018). It is clear, however, that schools of all types are complicit in a school-to-prison pipeline which disproportionately targets Black and brown children. In Atlanta Public

Schools, 80% of students are Black, but Black students account for 96% of out-of-school suspensions. In surrounding Fulton County Schools, in which Atlanta sits, Black students account for 42% of the total population but 81% of all out-of-school suspensions.

As is the case in many districts across the country, Black students are disproportionately suspended in every county in the Atlanta Metropolitan area (Stirgus & Albright, 2016). Additionally, a 2016 report from the Brookings Institution found corporal punishment was used on Black students in Georgia at twice the rate of their white counterparts (Startz, 2016). And though the Atlanta Police Department recently withdrew its officers from local schools, the school system maintains its own police department.

An April 2013 report by the Georgia Advisory Committee on behalf of the U.S. Commission on Civil Rights looked into Georgia's school discipline practices, noting the disparities and their correlation "with a greater likelihood of dropping out of school, which in turn often leads to eventual future incarceration," or what education experts across the country refer to as the "school-to-prison pipeline." Additionally, though the report did not look specifically at Atlanta, it did find a trend of over-referring Black students to alternative education programs for disciplinary violations. According to 2016 Census data, only 44.5% of Fulton County residents are Black, but Black youth make up 93% of the county's total intake for unique youth served for criminal offenses (School-to-Prison Pipeline, n.d.).

In the years immediately following the Civil War, Georgia ran "the most undiluted and typical form of convict leasing of any of the southern states" (Mancini, 1996). Convict leasing emerged as an answer to the South's new shortage of cheap labor following the abolition of slavery, and African Americans were arrested for what were mostly petty crimes—the most popular being vagrancy—and forced back into controlled labor by way of a loophole in the 13th Amendment which allowed forced labor as punishment for a crime. Nine in 10 of those leased out in this new system were Black (Forde & Bowman, 2017). Between 1872–1873, convict leasing generated more than $35,000 for the state of Georgia (Todd, 2014), or $674,455.34 in 2018 dollars.

Convict leasing would eventually give way to chain gangs, another system of forced prison labor. Historians describe both as an part of a systematic effort to reverse the progress made by Black citizens in the South during Reconstruction and maintain the intended social order of the South: one which would keep Black citizens from advancing and achieving equity in society.

"For some reason, there's this thinking that Black kids need to be trained, in terms of being Black children, as opposed to being human beings, whereas white kids deserve to be educated, in terms of being human beings, not in terms of their race," Johnson said.

The Impact of Gentrification

As Atlanta prepared to host the 1996 Olympics, city leaders made the decision to tear down the first publicly funded housing projects in Atlanta, sparking gentrification in the city, which would push most of Atlanta's Black residents out of downtown Atlanta.

In the process, communities were disrupted—"regardless of what people were telling you, they were communities," said Williams. At the same time, the city created a housing crisis that "then spun into cycles of school closures" and opened the door for more charter schools to come into the city while "pushing and pulling Black and brown people out of the city," Williams said. "It just created a lot of blight at the same time," he said.

Boarded up houses disrupt communities, open the door for investors to come in cheaply and sell to non-natives looking to relocate to the booming city, furthering the efforts to push poor Black and brown people out of the city. In many of the communities, the homeowners are not the people who live there, "they're speculators waiting for it to flip," according to Williams. "Here in Atlanta, our real estate is ripe for the taking," he said.

Though Atlanta hasn't had a White mayor since Maynard Jackson unseated incumbent mayor Sam Massell with 60% of the vote in 1973, the 2017 mayoral election saw the city come "very close to having a white mayor," which Williams said really "tells you something about the people in the city."

"I think there's a playbook for gentrification," said Williams. "There's some early adopters that just sort of move in because it's chic, then the next thing you see is a coffee house, then usually there's a really nice grocery store that opens up, and then they replace the [local school] principals with white principals" who then hire more white teachers. Meanwhile, many of the white students are re-zoned to neighboring school districts, like Fulton and Cobb county.

As a result, Atlanta Public Schools continues to produce students who are unprepared for life after high school. The school named for Alonzo Crim, the city's first Black superintendent and namesake of the center Williams heads, is a dropout factory, he said. Even students who manage to graduate from one of the schools on the city's south side are not set up for success in college.

A City "Full Of Colleges" Its Students Can't Access

"Atlanta is full of colleges, but I would say that not a majority of the people that come out of the school systems here can get into those colleges," said Sonja Roberts, an Atlanta native and Atlanta Metropolitan

State College's director of communications, who graduated from Atlanta Public Schools and knows well that many students with backgrounds like her own can be shut out of the city's better known institutions.

According to data (City Data), Georgia as a whole has the eighth lowest in-state enrollment in the country, with only 5.3% of its students comprising its higher education population. And APS students in particular score lower than their state-wide counterparts on important metrics—APS students averaged a 992 on the SAT in 2017 (McCray, 2017), which is lower than the state average of 1,050 and sits lower than the 1,030–1,230 requirement to get into Georgia State, for instance. And only 16 schools in the district even offer AP courses, often an indicator of college readiness.

Georgia State has received national attention for working to close the gap for students who are not prepared, and leaders credit early college programs—designed for students "on the bubble" to show them they can be successful in college.

Roberts is particularly proud to share 95% of students at Atlanta Metro are from the city of Atlanta and 65% are first-generation. "We meet students where they are and we take them beyond where they are to help them reach their potential—that's really what we're in the business of doing," she said.

A large part of meeting students where they are is understanding the circumstances facing the students and realizing that college success is more than just academic support. According to U.S. Department of Education data, of the 103 schools in APS, 94 are Title I-designated, signifying high percentages of low-income students in the school. And for students whose parents didn't go to college or don't make a lot of money, "it's very hard for students to see outside of that and break that cycle, and so the disparity continues," Roberts said.

"If they don't have access to education and then great education which then sets them up to have those grades that colleges are so strongly looking for to get in, and we know there's a correlation between income levels and how well you test—They don't have test prep," then it can seem like college is not an option for students, Roberts said. "I can't pay for it, I don't have the grades, and if I have the grades, I still can't pay for it, so what am I to do?"

And those challenges do not stop just because a student graduates from high school and matriculates to college.

"A majority of our students are Pell eligible and receive that aid, and we work with [a lot of] older students," said Roberts. "A lot of our students ride [Atlanta's public transit system,] MARTA. But that's very indicative of the financial status of these students—they don't have cars, they have to use public transportation."

As with many open-access institutions which admit high numbers of low-income students, these translate into additional challenges for the school's administration, as well. Most institutions today rely heavily on tuition dollars to keep the wheels turning, but at Atlanta Metro, a major selling point is the $16,000 four-year degree. It's a figure that's low enough to force administrators to be creative about figuring out how to keep things rolling, especially in the wake of enrollment declines facing the entire industry (when the economy is better, people don't go to college, Roberts said, reinforcing a well-known adage in higher education), but still high enough to be a challenge for some ("It's still $2,000 per semester that you don't have sitting around" if you're from a low-income household, she said).

"They don't understand the level of commitment coming in the door that it's going to take to go through two or four years of college, and because of the population, it's probably going to take them more time. Life gets in the way. They have families. Their housing is unstable, their food is unstable. So sometimes they have to go out to work for a semester, or it's too tough," she said, adding that they almost always come back. "They deal with things that would make any other person want to quit—quit at life—but they don't."

REFERENCES

Barnum, M. (2018, April 20). Do charter schools suspend students more? It depends on how you look at the data. Retrieved from https://www.chalkbeat.org/posts/us/2018/04/20/do-charter-schools-suspend-students-more-it-depends-on-how-you-look-at-the-data/

Forde, K. R., & Bowman, B. (2017, February 6). *Exploiting Black labor after the abolition of slavery.* Retrieved from https://theconversation.com/exploiting-Black-labor-after-the-abolition-of-slavery-72482

Georgia Colleges and Universities—Trade and Technical Schools. (n.d.). Retrieved from https://www.citytowninfo.com/places/georgia/colleges

Georgia School Discipline Report. (2013). Atlanta, GA: U.S. Commission on Civil Rights.

LEA Summary of Selected Facts. (n.d.). Retrieved from https://ocrdata.ed.gov/Page/PrintPage?t=d&eid=28846&syk=7&pid=2008&print=1&ct=c&pc=c

Mancini, Matthew J. (1996). *One dies, get another: Convict leasing in the American South,* 1866–1928. Columbia, SC: University of South Carolina Press. (Reviewed for EH.NET by Garland Brinkley, Department of Economics, School of Public Health, University of California-Berkeley.)

McCray, V. (2017, September 26). Atlanta Public Schools' SAT scores below state average. *Atlanta Journal-Constitution.* Retrieved from https://www.ajc.com/news/local-education/atlanta-public-schools-sat-scores-below-state-average/GTWpdlS8NMDHp6uehbq10N/

School-to-Prison Pipeline. (n.d.). Retrieved from http://www.project2ndchancega.org/school-to-prison-pipeline/

Startz, D. (2016, January 14). *Schools, Black children, and corporal punishment* (Rep.). Retrieved https://www.brookings.edu/blog/brown-center-chalkboard/2016/01/14/schools-Black-children-and-corporal-punishment/

Stirgus, E., & Albright, M. (2016, January 14). *Atlanta Journal-Constitution.* Retrieved from https://www.ajc.com/local-education/metro-atlanta-Black-students-suspension-rates/

Todd, W. A. (2014). Convict lease system. In *New Georgia Encyclopedia.* 10 January 2014. Web. 24 May 2018.

U.S. Census Bureau QuickFacts: Fulton County, Georgia. (n.d.). Retrieved from https://www.census.gov/quickfacts/fact/table/fultoncountygeorgia/PST045216

CHAPTER 2

BALTIMORE

INTRODUCTION

I have been an educator in Baltimore City for 15 years—straight out of undergraduate school. I had heard of Baltimore, but only through television. What I heard was nowhere near positive. My expectations of the city itself were low—I expected to enter an environment where drug dealers filled every corner, youth did not care about anything other than themselves and you had to watch your back because you could easily be shot down in broad daylight. Despite the low expectations for the city itself, my expectations of my scholars were extremely high. While I understood that their environments were not ideal, I expected them to want to be and do greater.

One day, one of my scholars—Robert, a deep thinking creative genius—picked up a book from my desk and exclaimed, "Mrs. Hall! You wrote this?" I excitedly shared with him that both books on my desk were not only authored by me but also available on Amazon, and one was an Amazon bestseller. He began to walk around the class showing the book to his peers, who were in disbelief and shock at the news. After he finalized his classroom tour, Robert shared with me an experience he had with a former English teacher. He said that the teacher promised to publish the work of the students in his class. The "publishing" was actually his work being stapled and placed in the main office for guests to review. He said he never tried again after that to write another story due to his disappointment.

Let's Stop Calling It an Achievement Gap, pp. 13–23
Copyright © 2019 by Information Age Publishing

Robert lived in a nice neighborhood, but was only a bed roll away from one of the most notoriously dangerous areas in the city. However, Robert was a stellar scholar: peaceful, soft-spoken; short and small in stature, he was a bushy haired kid who wrote poetry and practiced spoken word. Often the lines of his rhymes expounded upon the injustices he observed daily.

According to Merriam-Webster, the American Dream is thought of many Americans that something that can be achieved by working hard and becoming successful. I shared with my juniors at the Baltimore City high school I worked for that the American Dream can be transferred to illustrate my belief in them as an educator: a way of learning that can be achieved by any scholar in my classroom, especially by working hard and becoming successful.

These same scholars were to read and analyze Zora Neale Hurston's *Their Eyes Were Watching God* as a part of the Baltimore City Public School curriculum. The final Literacy Design Collaborative (LDC) essay required my scholars to discuss how the main character, Janie, attains her American Dream. My scholars participated in a plethora of activities to support their addressing the prompt: gallery walks, Think-Pair-Share discussions, Socratic seminars, and Kahoot-It games. These classroom-level connections led to my scholars entering challenging discussions in a safe atmosphere and sharing their own insights. To truly understand the definition of the American Dream, they should actually begin experiencing the vision of it.

The curriculum dictated that my scholars should write a five-paragraph essay that explained the ways in which the main character achieved her American Dream. We had classroom discussions and activities on this topic, but the pink elephant in the room seemed to be: Did my scholars know what their dream was? Was it American or based on their desire to leave Baltimore? What in the world could I do as a teacher to help them achieve anything at all other than a passing grade for an English credit? I thought about Robert and his excitement in knowing that I was a published author; that at one time in his life, he dreamed of doing the same. It was in that thought that I realized my true role and purpose in urban education.

I provided my scholars with safe, creative space to write a story from a modern perspective of someone their age who was attempting to reach their own American Dream. My scholars were engrossed in this project; they told their personal stories through the eyes of their fictional characters. Some shared that this task was therapeutic as they translated their inner thoughts, feelings, and emotions on paper. Others shared that they appreciated not only having to analyze the text but also having a say in how the story should develop. Some scholars were eager to share their stories, others were content in listening actively, nodding in approval at portions of the plot, snapping their fingers in support. In that moment, standing before a group of hopeful faces, I knew that I had a key that would unlock a door previously closed to their minds.

On May 27, 2016, a local news anchor brought his camera crew and interviewed my scholars, the young authors of *One Nation, One Heart*. My classroom had been transformed into an area for panelists and guests: tabled refreshments, a wall-sized banner signed by all the juniors sending congratulatory messages and best wishes to 35 newly published scholars. These scholars decided they not only wanted to write the story of the American Dream, but also benefit from their writing. Robert emotionally shared with the audience that he never thought that this day could be possible for him. His friend and fellow coauthor, Ahmad, expressed through tears that so many had doubted him and now he sat before the audience a published author. Collectively, the new authors earned over $1,000 in the sales of their books and untold numbers were inspired by their achievement and tenacity.

I believe that when you are great you have a responsibility to share that with others. After developing my own writing skills and becoming a bestselling author, I was more than happy to share the love of writing and publishing with my scholars. Now their book is also available on Amazon. The impact was not only great on my scholars, but also the community. A community member nominated their book for the national Indie Author's Legacy Award for Youth Authors of the Year—and they won! In one school year, my published, award-winning authors began to experience the American Dream.

Imagine if I had maintained the ideas that were taught to me of Baltimore youth through television and allowed those to dictate my expectations for my scholars. My experience in urban education has been excellent. I have met young people who wanted to learn and just needed a guide; kids who are afraid of what their future would hold but tenacious enough to push through and pursue all that was destined for them. Today, Robert is in college out of state, continuing in excellence. With the right words spoken over their lives, Robert and all Baltimore youth are the definition of success.

LaQuisha Hall is an English teacher at Carver Vocational-Technical High School in Baltimore City, and the Baltimore City Public Schools System's 2018 Teacher of the Year.

BALTIMORE

"Turning Trauma Into Power to Change the World"

When the Freddie Gray uprisings erupted in Baltimore in April of 2015, the nation watched, appalled. But few native to Baltimore would say they were surprised by what transpired during the 15-day protests and riots in response to the death of one of the city's sons after he sustained what would prove to be fatal injuries in the back of a police van. The tensions had been brewing for a long time. According to Baltimore native and historian Edwin T. Johnson, the dire conditions facing the city's West side had existed for generations, and as its residents sat by and watched others come to the city to access its harbor and waterfront amenities and its sporting events, anger grew as the residents were continually shut out of the jobs and economic development blooming just a mile East, across Martin Luther King, Jr. Ave. The anger, said Johnson, has long been "intensified by the backdrop of a poor relationship with the police department," which he says aids in restricting them from full citizenship and participation in their city.

Current Baltimore City Public Schools Superintendent Sonja Brookins Santelises said there's a public distrust of government institutions in the city in general, which includes the school systems. "There is still in Baltimore an overall need for institutional validity in the eyes of the public [to reinforce the idea] that we're called to serve, [and] as the head of the school system, I'm sensitive to that," she said.

In Baltimore, like other cities, education has become something that has been done to students, rather than with or for them. And the poor relationships with police and other city institutions are reflected in the public's relationship with the school system. "While Baltimore's public education system was not the cause of the city's condition after post-industrialization, [the city] was unprepared to counteract or address the conditions" facing its residents as industry turned, he says, and "the underground economy readily received young African American men who believed themselves to be out of options. The school system struggled to maintain relevance."

"Almost concurrent with election years is the discussion and threat of a state takeover of the Baltimore City system," says Johnson.

"The City That Reads"

Kurt Schmoke—the "pride of [Baltimore] City College" (Alvarez, 2016), a college preparatory high school, and the city's first African American mayor—declared his hometown "the city that reads" in a 1987 address. As Johns Hopkins University grew to become the city's biggest employer, Schmoke, who now serves as president of the University of Baltimore, said in a recent conversation that city officials realized they had "jobs that required a level of education and literacy that was different than what was required in the 1950s and '60s" when Baltimore was more of an industrial center.

The slogan quickly became a mockable decree, as illiteracy rates continue to rise and libraries across the city closed. According to 2016 PARCC data, 21% of the city's third graders were not reading on grade level—double the state average, according to the Baltimore Library Project (n.d.). The same year, city schools made headlines when it was discovered that five high schools and one middle school were found to have not a single student who scored proficient in math or reading (Papst, 2017).

"We had some financial issues that impacted the public school system that meant for many years, our system was underfunded and that meant that our students didn't get the kind of resources that they really needed," Schmoke said.

Those issues persist in many of the city's schools.

For generations, Baltimore City students have suffered an environment filled with violent crime, illiteracy, teenage pregnancy, single-parent families, sexually transmitted diseases, substance abuse, addiction and distribution, and teachers have been made to serve as social workers, psychologists, therapists and sociologists, Johnson said. Before they can attempt to educate, teachers and school leaders must first address the countless issues that their students carry with them to school each day.

Not only that, with grossly underfunded and under maintained buildings—today, you can't drink any of the water that comes out of any of the faucets in any Baltimore City school, because lead levels are too high—teachers have sometimes had to bring not just learning materials, but basic necessities like toilet paper for their students.

"One of the biggest challenges that the students in our public school system face is that we have a concentration of poverty in our city that is clearly not their fault but is another hurdle that they have to overcome," said Schmoke, who added that, as leader of the city's flagship university, "the message that we're trying to convey is that education will help them overcome that hurdle and some of the challenges."

The social-emotional needs of these students far outweigh those of students from more affluent school districts nearby, and their out-of-school support systems far less robust. Teachers are paid significantly less to deal with more, and as a result, Baltimore City has a 12.2% teacher attrition rate, significantly higher than the state's overall 7.1% average and second only to Prince George's County, the state's other urban district (Maryland State Department of Education, n.d.).

Today, Santelises, who grew up near and had most recently worked in Boston, says city officials are focusing on meeting the needs of the whole student, with a particular emphasis on "going very deep with literacy as the highest instructional leverage point and academic foundation." In other words, Baltimore is focusing on getting back to being the city that reads, a slogan Santelises says she wasn't familiar with when she sat down to identify system priorities.

She set her sights on building a culture around a focus on literacy as an empowerment tool—fluency is an educator's term, she said, but a message around "literacy for liberation, literacy for citizenship, literacy for agency and literacy to be able to bring your gifts, your talents and your insight for the collective good" resonates with the city's residents. Yes, early literacy and college readiness are important, she said, but what's more important to the citizens of Baltimore is voice, identity and influence and the idea of connecting your ideas to a broader audience.

Education should not only "expose young people to the world beyond what they see," it should also focus on "validating the strengths of their own identity," she said.

Refocusing District Priorities

Johnson calls the new Baltimore City School Headquarters, built in 2011, "a daily reminder of questionable spending practices and priorities within the system."

"The beautiful stately building is comparable to many of the historic edifices on the mall in Washington, D.C.," he says. But while the renovations of the headquarters were underway, the vast majority of school buildings in the district were in disrepair. "Most were built prior to the availability of central air conditioning and pose miserable conditions on hot days," he continued. "Old pipes fail and rupture regularly, and very few plumbing systems provide safe drinking water to water fountains. Many schools provide water that is safe for hand washing but unsafe for human consumption. Rodents, insects and other pests often attend classes more religiously than the students. The physical environment in many schools is far from conducive to learning and provides countless obstacles to academic achievement."

Take, for instance, Renaissance Academy, a public high school founded in 2005 which shares a building with Booker T. Washington Middle School. When the Baltimore Ravens gave Renaissance Academy $1.5 million in 2017 after reading about the condition of the school in the news and wanting badly to help, leaders of the high school dreamed of building a science lab, maybe restoring the gym floor. Instead, the money all went to building maintenance and renovation, with no budget from the district to cover the necessary costs. Santelises said the city is focusing on uncovering long-term structural issues with state funding, uncovering the current state of the district's school buildings and "the real precarious situation too many of our school buildings are still in" and moving the city forward. "In the midst of all of that uncovering deep-seated issues, we're going to have to address issues around equity," she said.

Perseverance, Resilience, Grit and Love

Nine students across the city were lost to violence in the 2017–2018 school year alone. Renaissance, like the students it serves, has seen more than its fair share of troubles. Former Ravens Safety, Ed Reed, who has volunteered with the school since he was drafted by the team in 2002, said during the ceremony unveiling the renovations that he'd seen 10 principals in his 15 years in the city. Just two years before, a student was fatally stabbed by a classmate on campus. The perpetrator was found not guilty, but he never returned to school, going out of state for a time to stay with family members, but never quite getting the support he needed, according to a mentor who had been working with him a few months before the incident. Despite the progress he made under the guidance of the mentor—the student had been reading at only about a first-grade level when the two were paired together, and he had reached about a fifth grade by the time the incident had occurred—the young man's fate had seemingly already been sealed years before by a system that had failed him at every level. He eventually returned to Baltimore and, at press time, was in jail again on unrelated charges, according to the mentor.

The school would lose two more students, both to off-campus incidents, within three months of the stabbing. Staff and students have rallied together in memory of their fallen classmates, and have found strength and power through their collective healing. The school's leaders have found art to be a good form of therapy, since many are apprehensive to see counselors— they don't trust adults in many cases, and the stigma that goes with seeing a counselor is not one anyone wants to own. But by the students' accounts, it is the love of their principal, Nikkia Rowe, which has kept them going.

After the shooting, Rowe and other administrators "went to people's houses, they called people, they did whatever they needed to do" to make sure the students and families knew the school was there for them, says Jasmine (student's first name is used only for privacy), a current senior at Renaissance. At one point, Jasmine had dropped out of school, over-whelmed by a number of things she was facing at home and feeling unable to juggle it all. Rowe reached out to her via Facebook messenger one day, noticing her prolonged absence, and told her to "come on back." She teared up as she talked about the interventions of her principal, who would send one of the school's administrators to pick her up if she was ever having a hard time making it to school, and who made sure she recovered all of her credits and walked across the stage in the Spring of 2018.

It occurred to the school community that if they put students at the center—something they say isn't really done in Baltimore City, particularly at the high school level—and brought in as many supports as possible to help students be successful during the day, to help move the needle for students. Community elders and leaders flock to the school, offering "stoop stories," guidance and mentorship to the students who walk its halls. Full-time mentors work with boys and girls in separate groups—and one-on-one for the boys, whom Rowe believes are particularly vulnerable.

"Many would prefer to assume that Renaissance Academy is the exception to the rule but we are not. We are the rule. Public education in America is stagnant and those in power refuse to respond to the evolving needs of students across the country, especially in urban school districts," wrote Rowe in a 2016 op-ed for *The Washington Post*. "There are schools all over the country fighting, just like Renaissance, to save the lives of children that society has consistently undervalued, hidden, and avoided," particularly young Black boys.

Rowe says she takes "a holistic approach to loving and educating and empowering kids," but realizes they still face challenges and influences outside of school that are beyond her control. "There are kids who have gone onto college, four-year college, came back, shot out the windows [damaging school property]," and landed themselves in jail, but as soon as they're able, they've run right back to Renaissance—the only place they know to go—asking for help with restorative services, she said.

"This is definitely the safe space," says Jasmine, who laments the closure of many of the recreation centers and the lack of opportunities and activities for youth in the city, saying, "when I leave here, it's like where am I going?" Other students agree that more jobs in the city are needed to give youth something to do when they aren't in school to keep them out of trouble. State's Attorney Marilyn Mosby's Project 17 youth work initiative seeks to "reduce chronic absence and truancy through employment," and students say it has made a tremendous impact, but there still are not enough jobs for everyone.

Meanwhile, in a continued testament to the great divide in the opportunities afforded residents in West Baltimore versus cross-city counterparts, a 235-acre, $5.5 billion project is underway to build a mini city anchored by Under Armour's new world headquarters just over four miles away, concentrating all of the wealth, resources and opportunities in an area that will remain shut off to the students and families Renaissance serves.

Progress Comes Slowly

The efforts of Renaissance's leadership team are paying off, but slowly. There remains a 60% chronic absentee rate in the school, but students are absent fewer days, a remnant of the Freddie Gray uprisings, when school attendance across the city hit the floor. But whereas students may have missed 30 school days two years ago, today the same students may miss only 10—progress that isn't reflected in blanket statistics about absenteeism, just as one student's progress from a first-grade reading level to fifth in a few months is not reflected in overall literacy statistics. Two years in a row, the school was scheduled for closure by the district, and each time the students and families showed up at the school board meetings and convinced the district's leadership to reconsider.

But Renaissance, like every other school in the city, is a community school—an initiative of the school board which precedes Santelises's arrival and prioritized making sure every school has "systems, structures, processes and resources in place to be able to link the resources of the community to the needs of our young people and vice versa: to take the needs of our young people into account with the resources that our city can provide," Santelises said. There is a focus on mapping resources based on historic redlining maps to determine where people are historically underfunded. "Schools really belong to communities. We have, for a variety of reasons, we have unfortunately made schools institutions in the middle of the communities, when they really are extensions of the community," she said. And a number of corporate and philanthropic partners have stepped up to say "we want to help," which Santelises said is a positive result of making public one's agenda.

Officials and community members are confident Baltimore will persevere. "People of color, trauma is in our DNA," says Larry Simmons, a program manager at the Baltimore City Health Department who also works closely with Renaissance, who adds the focus should be on "celebrating the assets [and resiliency] that come out of making trauma a part of our DNA."

REFERENCES

Alvarez, R. (2016, November 4). Resurrecting 'The City that Reads'. *Baltimore Sun*. Retrieved from http://www.baltimoresun.com/news/opinion/oped/bs-ed-alvarez-1106-20161105-story.html

Baltimore: Poverty, Children, Literacy … & Libraries. (n.d.). Retrieved June 23, 2018, from https://www.baltimorelibraryproject.org/plot/baltimore-poverty-children-literacy/

Papst, C. (2017, May 17). 6 Baltimore schools, no students proficient in state tests. *Fox 45 News*. Retrieved from http://foxbaltimore.com/news/project-baltimore/6-baltimore-schools-no-students-proficient-in-state-tests

Teacher Attrition. (n.d.). Maryland State Department of Education. Retrieved from https://wcp.k12lds.memsdc.org/webcenter/faces/oracle/webcenter/page/scopedMD/sacc1b19d_f243_4591_9224_dc0ebf1851b8/Page26.jspx;jsession id=ZlCpbYGSvd70wh2sv0QVJLV1P0Swt3PMTF7Xnm8W8Qgmzhn1xknJ!1 357877685!NONE?wc.contextURL=/spaces/ts&_adf.ctrl-state=14y5a9qq9 9_4&scope=ts&visibility=visible&_afrLoop=4688123395579740#@?scop e=ts&visibility=visible&_afrLoop=4688123395579740&wc.contextURL=/ spaces/ts&_adf.ctrl-state=1bzvbe2a2w_4

CHAPTER 3

BIRMINGHAM

INTRODUCTION

The Birmingham City School system has changed a great deal since I was a student in the 50s. When I started school in 1952, the Black students had their neighborhood schools and the White students had their neighborhood schools.

When I was in school, the teachers had time for all the students and worked hard to get all students to learn, even though there might have been 30, 35, or 40 students in a class. Still, the Black teachers in the Black schools were caring and worked very hard to educate the students. In other words, the teachers were professionals and they cared about their jobs and the students they were hired to teach. In the '50s and '60s, when I was in school, all the students had textbooks. We were taught in English class the parts of speech which was a part of the curriculum in the '50s and '60s. I learned in my English class about nouns, pronouns, adjectives, verbs, and so forth. We also learned how to speak. When I was in elementary school, the girls took Home Economics to learn how to cook and sew, the boys had carpentry class. When I was in school, principals took their jobs seriously—they came to classrooms and observed how and what the teachers were teaching.

Let's Stop Calling It an Achievement Gap, pp. 25–34
Copyright © 2019 by Information Age Publishing
All rights of reproduction in any form reserved.

We didn't have a lot of resources—at one time, the parents had to purchase the books from a bookstore. A few years later, the school system started furnishing the books.

When the laws changed and Birmingham City Schools had to abide by the laws of the land and the schools had to be integrated, many things changed. The majority of the Black schools still had a majority of Black teachers and the White schools had mostly White teachers. By the time my children started school, there were a few White teachers in the Black schools and a few Black teachers in the White schools. The White teachers were in the schools to do a job; it was up to you to learn what they were teaching. Some of the Black teachers—especially the older ones—still cared about doing whatever they could to teach the students. In other words, the White teachers were not as concerned or caring about the Black students. I am not saying that all White teachers had a problem teaching the Black students, but some did.

When my children were in school, the classes had approximately 30 students in a class. When my children were in school, the district furnished the text books.

Today, in my grandchildren's classes, if there are 20 to 25 students in a class the teachers say they have too many students in the class.

Today, we have some books for the high school students and in the elementary and middle schools, some of the students have books and some do not. Some of the subjects that are being taught are taught on the computer. The students have workbooks that they carry home instead of hardback books. I am aware of the fact that we are now in the computer and digital age, but some of our students today are having a hard time learning how to read, do math, and perform in other subjects. Some of our teachers do not go that extra mile to find out what is going on with the students outside of the classroom.

Things have really changed in the education arena. Very few of the students in our school system know anything about English Literature, or how to write an essay. Neither my children or grandchildren have had English classes that have prepared them to write or speak correctly. Students today do not know what it is to actually learn poems or to read Shakespeare. I doubt if any of my grandchildren could tell you any poems by William W. Longfellow or Edgar Allen Poe.

Today, we have Career Technical classes, which were in the schools when both my children and grandchildren were attending Birmingham City Schools. The idea behind career tech is to prepare you for a job in the future if you are not planning to go to college. The down side of this is that all schools do not offer the same classes.

I would say few principals actually know what is going on in the classrooms today. Principals and teachers were respected by the students when my generation was in school; today it is quite different. Some of the principals and teachers are more focused on getting higher degrees and making more money than they are on making sure the students are being taught and getting the education they need to succeed in life.

Another thing that has changed is the parent involvement. Years ago, if a student was involved in any type of sports or other school activity, the parents came out to support the students. Today, very few parents attend basketball, football or theatrical productions in our school district. They do very little to support the programs financially, which was totally different in the past. In our system, it is very hard to get parents or teachers involved in the PTA. The majority of today's parents have 9–5 jobs and cannot come to a meeting in the daytime, and teachers do not want to come back to the schools for an evening meeting.

One reason our school system has had so many changes is that we have had some major administrative changes, accompanied by lots of turnover through the years. Prior to 1983, all Birmingham City School Superintendents were White. In 1983, Birmingham City Schools had their first Black superintendent (interim). With this change came many changes in our district office and classrooms. In 1988, the district got our first Black superintendent, with more administrative changes.

Since then, we have had 12 superintendents and six interim superintendents. Each time we have had changes in leadership, this has created administrative changes and changes in the classrooms.

Today, we have to realize that we have a different breed of parents, students and teachers. Until we face reality and understand what is needed in our classrooms, we will not be able to do the work that is needed to get our students prepared for today's society.

I still personally believe that getting an education in the Birmingham City School System in the '50, '60, and '70s was much better than it is today.

Mrs. Sandra K. Brown is the District 9 representative of the Birmingham City Schools Board of Education, currently in her second term. She is a product of Birmingham City Schools and her three children and eight grandchildren have also matriculated through the system. Mrs. Brown is the former President of the North Birmingham Neighborhood Community as well as former Vice President of the Birmingham Citizen Advisory Board.

BIRMINGHAM

"Segregation Forever" and the Impact
of Suburban Flight

When George Wallace promised "segregation now, segregation tomorrow and segregation forever" in his inaugural address after he was elected
governor of Alabama in 1963, he was not just responding in defiance to the
"tyranny" that was court-ordered integration in the '60s—he was perhaps
laying out a mandate for life in Alabama for decades to follow.

The deliberateness of the city and the district to maintain segregation
has been challenged in court numerous times. In 1957, Reverend Fred
Shuttlesworth led a group of parents petitioning the city to provide educational accommodations for their children close to their homes. They were
met by a notice from then State Superintendent of Education Austin Ruel
Meadows admonishing them to respect the decision of the superintendent
and members of the board to place the children as they saw fit, and notify-
ing them that citizens of the state had voted to change the Constitution
to "abolish the right of education or training of any individual at public
expense."

Further, the notice said, pursuant to a vote by the citizens of Alabama,
"any public school and all public schools can be abolished and the school
buildings can be rented or given to individuals to operate private schools. If
you refuse to cooperate with the city board of education in the school placement of your children, you will in effect invite the abolishment of the public
schools. Where would your children be, and where would the children of
your friends and your people be in this State without public schools?"

The district built new all-Black schools to combat attempts to integrate, ignoring the mandate in *Brown vs. Board of Education* and moving on with the promise of "segregation forever" (Loder-Jackson, 2015). Magnet schools were created as an alternative to cross-town bussing.

Today, a number of advocates and Black education officials in Birmingham, Montgomery and other seminal cities that once served as backdrops for key moments in the Civil Rights Movement would say segregation remains a top issue for students in the state. Tondra Loder-Jackson, director of the Center for Urban Education at the University of Alabama at Birmingham wrote in 2015 that education in the city, most known for its role in the civil rights movement to advance equity, today is much more reflective of the "separate but equal" doctrine of *Plessy vs. Ferguson* than the inclusive spirit of *Brown vs. Board of Education* (Loder-Jackson, 2015).

Birmingham has been a continual site for lawsuits to integrate schools —many of which U.W. Clemon, Alabama's first Black federal judge, and a former lawyer and legislator who sued Paul "Bear" Bryant's football team over integration and continually challenged Governor George Wallace as a state senator, has been involved with in some capacity. "We're still very much involved in litigation," decades after *Brown v. Board* made desegregation the law of the land, he said.

These lawsuits, and continuing debates over integration in general, were never about an idea that Black students were better off if they could be around White students, they were about the idea that Black students would be better off if they could have access to the same education that White students had. But even when there are not actual policies in place to enforce school segregation, residential segregation—and policies that allow district lines to be drawn around neighborhood lines—still enables de facto school segregation.

"Magic Boxes" to Uphold Segregation

In Jefferson County, which houses Birmingham, there are 27 different municipalities, and 12 different school districts, thanks to a state law that allows locales to break out and form their own school districts, as long as they have 5,000 people and a municipality that can fund it.

"We have a lot of school districts that have pulled out and kind of drew those magic boxes to form their own school districts, and a lot of times minority students were cut out of those districts, whether intentional or not," said Orletta Rush, who serves as director of special initiatives for Jefferson County Public Schools.

The county is still under a 50-year federal desegregation order, and as such, Clemon said Jefferson County Schools have "pretty much achieved the student desegregation numbers that is should have achieved," though there is still work to be done to achieve parity with teachers and administrators. "Jefferson County has this prevailing policy of deferring to local principals for the selection of faculty and staff—most principals are White, so most new hires" are also White, he said.

But for other districts in the county, particularly those predominantly Black districts left by the creation of other, smaller municipal districts, "the education is likely to remain inadequate and inferior," Clemon said, because they are no longer under any federal mandate to ensure equity. The fundamental issue remains one of disparate resources.

In Jefferson County, as each predominantly White, more affluent neighborhood has pulled out and formed its own school district, it has taken with it the resources—via both property taxes and parent contributions—that make schools better for all students in the city. And Black students have suffered the most.

"You just have so many of these little pockets, and you have the haves who have pulled their students to the side and got their resources just for their students. And you see the ones that are struggling, the ones that are high poverty, high minority," said Rush. "It just puts a lot of barriers within the community to absorb," and usually in those which can't afford to absorb the deficits.

To comply with desegregation orders, the suburban districts poach the top athletes and best students from Birmingham City and other predominantly Black districts, creating "a lot of fragmented districts" and leaving the home districts in an even more vulnerable position, said long-time Birmingham resident and Bessemer City Middle School staff member Tristan Twyman.

Separate but Equal?

Birmingham City has made a number of efforts to level this out via voter referenda to increase various taxes to provide additional funding. Thanks to what Twyman calls an exceptional capital improvement program, every school in the city has seen improvements to facilities in recent years, from remodeling to wing additions to complete rebuilding—even those that are under enrolled, according to Twyman.

Twyman also said the city and district should be credited for making sure every school has music, band, art, foreign language, counseling, libraries, physical education, and other enrichment programs that have been cut in many places across the country, and students as young as kindergarten have the opportunity to take these classes. Students have the opportunity to select public high schools based on their programs of interest, and there are a plethora of offerings in the city's public schools, he said.

Seventy-nine percent of Birmingham City Schools teachers are African American, and 93% of them meet the No Child Left Behind standard of "highly qualified."

But the offerings don't always necessarily match the experience, he said. There are a lot of transient teachers, which makes it difficult to ensure the consistency of the offerings at each school, and in many cases, staff members are shared between schools or grade levels. There are K–8 schools that may have 13 teachers for the whole school, he said. And there may be schools that have one social studies teacher for both seventh and eighth graders, versus separate seventh and eighth grade teams.

While teacher positions may be stretched thin, Twyman said there is a lot of duplication and bloat in the administrative structure of the district. "It's still run as if we have 75,000 students," with multiple individuals holding the same titles with oversight of different clusters he said, despite the fact that demographic changes and suburban flight have left district enrollment hovering right around 25,000 students. Student retention remains challenging, Twyman said. Henig, Hula, Orr, and Pedescleaux (1999) acknowledged in their work that schools in Black-led cities face similar challenges as schools in White-led cities, but found "race is particularly salient in understanding a city's capacity to garner necessary civic support for urban schools." And Loder-Jackson (2015) said even well-intentioned school reformers lack the emotional and fiscal commitment to the welfare of urban schools, particularly once they're perceived to be the responsibility of the Black "elite" elected or appointed to govern those districts, which dooms these leaders to fail due to nonexistent support structures.

Black middle-class families have also lost faith in the system, which was overtaken by the state in 2012 amid fiscal and administrative challenges and accreditation probation warnings, according to Loder-Jackson (2015). A number of school board members in 2012 sued then-Superintendent Craig Witherspoon, who they said was doing the bidding of the White business and civic communities "at the expense of the livelihoods of African American school personnel and the best interests of the community and students" (Loder-Jackson, 2015). Student achievement, finances and high school graduation rates have all increased, but Twyman said those gains have gone unnoticed.

Even as Birmingham City Schools make improvement, "the district isn't moving fast enough to keep up" with the suburban districts, and any gains it does make are overshadowed by those nearby, according to Twyman.

Despite greater gains in standardized tests and other metrics, "The suburban schools outshine Birmingham schools all day long," Twyman said. "The suburban schools are seen as better, even when they may not necessarily be, they're seen as better because of where they are, the makeup of those communities." There is no context given to the different starting points of students in the district or any recognition that the content knowledge and background knowledge is very different for the different populations, he said.

And the way the schools are publicly portrayed varies along the same lines. "You can have a suburban school that has police that come to the school every day for the same kind of problems you'd have in the city school, but the city school is going to catch much more flack for it than the suburban schools," said Twyman, who pointed out that the students at both schools are the same age and prone to the same types of bad decisions. "You may never hear of the police going to the suburban school, but the city school is going to make the news. And the accomplishments of our city schools kind of get downplayed in light of the suburban schools. You can have our city schools make gains on standardized tests, but it's looked at as 'you're still not as good as the other kids.' "

The perception bleeds over into perceived prestige of the jobs as well, he said—if one works in Birmingham City, s/he is seen as inferior to those who work in the suburban districts.

In-Fighting Leads to Lack of Investment

The in-fighting, even among Black leaders and members of the Black middle class has led to a lack of investment and coalition-building in the district, according to Loder-Jackson, who said the lack of large-scale coalition building between Black educators, parents and community members "runs counter, historically, to the coalitions in Birmingham which fought for educational equity in the 19th and 20th centuries" (Loder-Jackson, 2015). But Black citizens are even more leery of coalitions which include White frontmen and women from more affluent communities, and remain distrustful that these leaders have the best interest of Black students and families in mind, believing instead the coalitions are only "Trojan horses mounted to drive in a new wave of White control and power-brokering in the city's schools as well as selected inner-city neighborhoods deemed profitable to long-range downtown economic development" (Loder-Jackson, 2015).

For those White "social entrepreneurs" who are interested in enacting change, Loder-Jackson (2015) said it is important that they make sure they're working with, not around, the residents of the city in deciding what's best for their children. Otherwise, they risk invoking the spirit of Meadows when he told Shuttlesworth and the cadre of Black parents to "cooperate with the decision of the local board of education to place your child in the school they think will be best for your child."

REFERENCES

Henig, J. R., Hula, R. C., Orr, M., & Pedescleaux, D. S. (1999). *The color of school reform: Race, politics, and the challenge of urban education.* Princeton, NJ: Princeton University Press.

Loder-Jackson, T. L. (2015). *The sociopolitical context of education in post-civil rights Birmingham. Peabody Journal of Education, 90*(3), 336–355. doi:10.1080/0161 956x.2015.1044288

CHAPTER 4

CHARLOTTE

INTRODUCTION

The slogan that I constantly see posted on Charlotte-Mecklenburg Schools literature proudly states "Every Child, Every Day, For A Better Tomorrow." The slogan gives the notion that the goal of Charlotte-Mecklenburg Schools is to serve each child daily in such a manner that they will have the opportunity to achieve the goal of having a better future by receiving a quality education in their system. A recent study proves that slogan to be false. Charlotte is ranked 50th out of 50 major U.S. cities for upward mobility for students who live in poverty (Chetty, Hendren, Kline, & Saez, 2014). Students in poverty have a 4.4% chance of getting out of poverty in our city. This plays a direct part in our students not being prepared when they complete their educational journey in Charlotte-Mecklenburg Schools. When I say our students, I am talking about Black students.

Charlotte-Mecklenburg Schools uses many descriptive words to dance around using the word Black when referring to students: at-risk, high poverty, lower performing, and my new favorite, low SES, which stands for low socioeconomic status.

For a school district to pride itself on reaching every child every day, it continues to prove itself wrong based on the results of the students' performance. Black students continue to perform lower than their White counterparts on the end of the year tests. White students continue to grad-

Let's Stop Calling It an Achievement Gap, pp. 35–45
Copyright © 2019 by Information Age Publishing
All rights of reproduction in any form reserved.

uate at a higher rate than Black students. Something is wrong with the system as a whole. Every child is being served in Charlotte-Mecklenburg Schools every day, but how they are being served is a different experience and it does not lead to a better tomorrow for many Black students.

When I attended elementary school in Charlotte-Mecklenburg Schools back in the 1980s, I was bussed from my neighborhood to attend Shamrock Gardens Elementary, a school with large tress, front porches with tall White columns around the corner from the prominent Charlotte Country Club. As I think back on the busing experience, the majority of the students who were being bussed were Black students to White neighborhoods. As a child, I didn't mind. Shamrock Gardens was a K–3 school. The diversity I experienced at this school was great for social development. I attended school with students from different races, different income levels, and different neighborhoods. If I never learned one multiplication fact while I was there, I received a lesson in how to act and interact with many different people who did not look, act, talk, and think like me. Even the teachers and administration were diverse. During my time there I had Black, White, female, male teachers and principals. As a child in my developmental stage of life, it was a priceless lesson.

After completing third grade, I was no longer bussed across town. I had the pleasure of walking to school with everyone else in my neighborhood. I attended school at Oaklawn Elementary School, which was a few blocks from our home and served students from Grades 4–6. The bus ride to Shamrock Gardens was fun, but the walk to and from Oaklawn Elementary with my friends every day was far better. All the neighborhood kids from Oaklawn Ave., McCrorey Heights, Washington Heights, Pitts Drive, Kenny Street, Dundeen, Booker Ave. Waddell Park, and Russell Ave. all were going to school in the neighborhood. Even though we all went to Shamrock Gardens together, going to Oaklawn seemed different. Some of my other Black and White friends that I met that lived on the east side of Charlotte were not bussed to our school. We had some White students bussed in to Oaklawn, but most of those who were bussed in were Black students from the east side of Charlotte. The school was still diverse, but it was not as diverse as my previous school.

When it was time for me to attend junior high school, my mother entered me into what I now know was the beginning of the massive lottery system we have now in our school system composed of several magnet schools. The two options at that time for the lottery were Hawthorne Traditional and Piedmont Open. I was accepted to Hawthorne Junior High, and it turned out to be by far the best experience I had in my K–12 years. This school was a diverse mix of students from all over the county. This is where my educational experience of learning how to achieve in an academic setting began. How to interact with Black and White students from all around the county, because Hawthorne was close to being 50:50 when it came to the ratio of Black:White students. It felt that way to me, even if it wasn't. I excelled in sports. I developed friendships which persist to this day. Hawthorne was the perfect example of how education is supposed to be: Strong academic rigor along with a diverse mix of racial and economic students who are constantly interacting with one another positively. We still have Hawthorne Junior High School reunions to this day.

My high school years were different. I left Charlotte-Mecklenburg Schools and attended a prominent private school in Charlotte, Charlotte Country Day School. There was no diversity. Most of the students who attended this school came from affluent, rich families and had only gone to school with those type of people all of their lives. They really did not understand life outside of their rich, affluent world. They referenced kids who attended Charlotte-Mecklenburg Schools as "those public school kids." They used reference points designed to prove they know what it is it like to be poor or Black because they have a Black friend or have been in contact with poor or Black people who worked at their parents' companies, but these references only served to draw a deeper divide between the groups.

Those memories reflect what the public schools of Charlotte-Mecklenburg Schools have become at opposite ends. Schools in Charlotte-Mecklenburg have become schools made up of schools with no diversity and they have no reference point of what it is like to interact with students who do not look, talk, act or speak like them.

As a parent, I decided to place my children in magnet schools. The schools they have attended offered the opportunity to go to school with a diverse group of children from all over the county. Our neighborhood school was not an option for them, based on the reputation and test scores.

As an advocate for Black students in the Charlotte-Mecklenburg Schools, I have learned that the Black neighborhood schools do not have the same educational experience as other schools in the county. In the Black neighborhoods, a number of elementary and middle schools have been closed down and students were forced to attend K–8 schools. Elementary schools that were built to serve elementary-aged students now served students who were in middle school. It is nothing for an eighth grader to use a bathroom with a kindergartner.

Athletics, arts, and foreign languages were removed from these schools and the schools have been stripped to the bare minimum. Schools are overcrowded and use trailers to compensate for the overcrowding. In the high schools in these same neighborhoods, students were not offered the same advanced courses as students attending schools that were predominantly White. If students wanted to take an advanced class, they would have to take a virtual class and learn online. The high schools implemented credit recovery programs to help failing students get caught up by sitting in front of computer and answering a few questions, allowing that to suffice to catch them up on any material they may have missed or failed in previous years. It is an easy way to give diplomas to students and keep graduation rates high, but these Black students don't leave prepared for life after high school.

I have noticed that Charlotte Mecklenburg-Schools is a separate and unequal school system. Poor kids do not receive the same opportunities as wealthy kids. Black kids do not receive the same opportunity as White kids. Black kids are not treated the same as White kids. Black students make up 40% of the district, but comprise 80% of the suspensions district wide (Helms, 2017). It seems as if Black students are not wanted in the school system or the system does not care. If the community recognizes the disparities in how Black students are treated, then I know the students recognize it. It is hard to perform in an environment that seems hostile and makes you feel you are not wanted. That is why Black students are not performing at the same level as their White counterparts.

Gregory "Dee" Rankin is a Charlotte native who attended Charlotte-Mecklenberg schools and has children in the system. He currently serves as the Chair of the Education Committee of the Black Political Caucus of Charlotte Mecklenburg where he advocates for all youth in Charlotte-Mecklenburg Schools especially Black students. He is founder and Executive Director of Future L.E.A.D.E.R.S. of NC, a nonprofit designed to empower youth in the region to improve academic achievement and pursue success in chosen careers.

CHARLOTTE

"The Fleecing of the Urban School District"

Charlotte, like most other cities, had tried busing as a response to the landmark *Brown v. Board of Education* verdict. But former Charlotte-Mecklenburg Schools Board Member Arthur Griffin (1999) has long wondered why only Black students were bussed, and only Black schools closed. "Why are we busing all these little early preschool Black kids, when the court order said to bus some white kids at some point," he asked in a recorded interview with Pamela Grundy as part of an oral history project for the University of North Carolina.

Griffin, who was not interested in education at the time, had taken an internship with the Legal Aid Society in the mid-70s and was disturbed by the number of Black parents who were coming in seeking help in the proceedings of their children, who had been suspended without conference from their schools. The Society did not get involved with education, so he took it upon himself to independently represent the families as a paralegal.

"I remember at West Charlotte, specifically, a young White male—well, first, it was called a big riot, it was in the newspaper that Black and White kids were fighting. And some of the parents contacted me, because some of the kids weren't going to be able to graduate because of the disciplinary hearings. I went up to the school to represent some of the kids, and during my investigation, I talked with most of the participants, and then at the very hearing, the White male student said, 'I started the fight. I didn't like what he said,' or he thought the kid said, and, 'Yeah, I walked across and I hit him and we went through the window and my boys got into it and his boys got into it,' " Griffin said in the interview. When he asked the White student if he had given the same account to the principal at the time of the incident, the student said he had. Griffin realized that the principal had suspended the Black student despite evidence that the Black student did not start the fight and thought "that was just patently unfair," he said in the interview.

But it wasn't uncommon. In a phone interview, Griffin said for Black students in the district, "If you looked at the teacher wrong, you were sent home. There was no opportunity for [you or your parents] to challenge that decision of the school," he said.

These issues persist today. A 2017 analysis by the Charlotte Observer found Black students in Charlotte-Mecklenburg Schools are nine times more likely than their White counterparts to be suspended. And though Black students in Charlotte-Mecklenburg Schools are suspended at a rate that mirrors the suspension rate in the state as a whole, White students in CMS schools are less likely to be suspended than their peers around the state (Helms, 2017).

Once students were back in school, there were still more issues to address. "'Ok, you got my kid back in school, but it looks like he's not going to graduate, he's failing,'" he said. "So I started looking at why are these kids not being successful academically. ... I was continually discovering that the adequate resources were not being provided for our kids."

When the Leandro family argued before the North Carolina Supreme Court in 1997 that the quality of a child's education should not be dependent on the wealth of the family, the court unanimously ruled that neither districts nor counties were constitutionally obligated to provide equal funding. However, the justices decided, the state of North Carolina was responsible for providing "a sound basic education" to all students, guaranteeing their ability to read, speak English, and have "sufficient fundamental knowledge" of physical science, geography, history, and basic economic and political systems. The state is also to guarantee each student's "sufficient academic and vocational skills" to ensure every student can fully engage in postsecondary or vocational opportunities, and compete with other students on a national scale in those pursuits (*Leandro v. State*, 1997).

However, Griffin pointed out, the original plaintiff has graduated from high school, received a bachelor's degree and a law degree and the state has still not figured out how to deal with the *Leandro* ruling.

Erik Turner, who currently serves as principal of Sedgefield Middle School, said "for African American students, particularly those who live in under resourced areas, their educational experience is a segregated educational experience—segregated by socioeconomic status and also by race."

Turner said he finds this fact "frustrating, because our city, at one point, was a national model for integration."

A "Retreat" From Desegregation Efforts

Griffin said that as a nation, "We never completed the journey from *Brown* when we were trying to eradicate separate and unequal." The nation made an effort to correct the disparities through funding increases and attempts to improve the efforts to get Black students equitable resources in the '60s and '70s in the wake of *Brown*, he said, but once Ronald Reagan took office, "there was a retreat" from this imperative, "and we've been retreating ever since."

"Whether it's having highly qualified teachers in the classroom, whether having diversity of your classroom teachers, it could be a lack of resources, in terms of just cash funding, the issue of the day could be we don't have adequate resources to buy technology or resources, it could be that we have a real shortage of qualified teachers," said Griffin, who pointed out that when there's a shortage of anything, Black schools are the ones which suffer the shortages. "In the '70s in Charlotte we had skills classes on the bottom which taught low-level math, low-level English, and I was concerned with why are all the Black kids, or the majority of Black kids in these low-level skill classes. Where are the opportunities not being provided for our youngsters," Griffin said.

Charlotte historian Tom Hanchett, in a recent discussion of gentrification and urban renewal in Charlotte, said of historic patterns in the city, "African Americans had almost no say in what was going to happen to their neighborhood. If you were an important leader and you wanted to do something, well, heck, do it right through the middle of the Black neighborhood—because nobody's going to complain" (Oyler, 2018).

The same formula and thinking could be copy-pasted into any city and district in the country. Thanks to the combination of gentrification and a retreat away from intentional efforts to remedy the vestiges of segregated education, Turner said "re-segregation in the city has spread and has really contributed to the limited opportunities" for Black and brown students.

"All of my kids are poor Black and brown, but I'm in the heart of the city in a neighborhood that doesn't look like my school," he said.

Finding a Fix

Griffin said as school board president, his approach was to identify desired outcomes without getting mired down into strategies. "In education, there's lots of buckets to try to fix holes, but you never fix the leak.

And we don't have enough buckets to stop the leaks. You have to fix the holes. And that takes leadership," he said.

So Griffin's school board set out to focus on two goals: First, every high school student would successfully take an Advanced Placement (AP) class. This provided a national benchmark to which to compare students in Charlotte-Mecklenburg schools to others across the country, and it quietly achieved the goal of getting more Black students into AP classes without having to get into the debate about how schools would pay for AP textbooks, which cost twice as much as regular textbooks. Second, every third-grader would know how to read. "It's a lot less expensive to fix a second grader who can't read than an 11th grader," he said.

"I tried to get smart and rather than point out these disparities as a philosophical debate, I started to say I want to set these goals for the system," said Griffin, who had previously pointed out that bringing up conversations about racism and disparities had been "taboo" in Charlotte's "polite society." "I was saying here's the goal, here's the outcome for all students, now you figure out how to get there."

The efforts paid off— sort of. Griffin said at one point, one-third of all African American children who took AP exams in the state and over one-quarter of all African American students who passed the exam came out of Charlotte, despite the district accounting for only 8% of the state's Black enrollment. But, he said, "we had like a 72% graduation rate."

"We did a poor job during my tenure, in terms of high school graduation—we were so focused on making sure third graders knew how to read that we didn't focus enough on the high school students," he said. "When you don't have enough resources, you have to make a decision," and in the case of Charlotte-Mecklenburg students, those decisions led to the sacrificing of the older students who cost more to remediate.

"There should have been smaller classes at the high school level. There should be 10 kids in a class if they can't read, with a reading teacher to help them—but that's a funding issue. And most districts can't afford that around the country," said Griffin.

In spite of this admitted failure, he feels the district did a very good job between 1998–2004 of making sure students were learning. "We have a tendency to not look holistically at what does the educated child look like? What does a successful graduate look like," he asked. Griffin is pleased that across the country, Black students are graduating at a higher rate than they've ever graduated, and Charlotte is no exception. However, he feels the gains can easily slip.

"When you lose your focus, you're back to '78 instead of being in 2018. It's a cycle. And where some people at this one time are focused on this one thing," it's easy to lose sight of all of the other important factors that go into educating a child, he said.

Impact of Culture

One of those things, said Turner, is school culture and its intertwining with neighborhood culture and the culture of the students it seeks to serve.

"When you start talking about school culture and what a school can do to create a culture of engagement, some of the challenges that we present are the same cultures of the neighborhood," he said. "The law and rule of the neighborhood will become the law and rule of the school."

This can be a challenge if the law and rule of the neighborhood is violence, and in many urban schools, Turner believes this is what accounts for a lot of teacher turnover. "School improvement is a challenge, because it takes a different skill set, and what we're finding is that what's being taught in our traditional teacher education programs is not enough," he said.

"Relationship-building is huge and also the cultural competencies" piece and finding ways to not devalue "the cultural currency that our kids bring into the building, but [identifying] how do we take the cultural currency that they bring and take that and transfer it into a skill," he said.

For example, "Our kids have much more grit than kids who come from better resources," Turner continued. He also said it's important not to focus so much on teaching students to code switch to assimilate—we don't want you to "leave everything you know and value at the door," he said, but as educators, it is your job to "articulate that as a transferable skill" and "acknowledge and articulate that what you bring in has value."

And for school leaders, there is a responsibility to train staff to know and think this way as well, scaffolding the support and the interventions used in the building in a way that resonates with the students, even when they don't jive with what's taught in traditional teacher education programs.

For example, understanding the dynamics between language, power, and cultural expression goes a long way in how an educator manages his or her classroom. "If in the neighborhood, I have to be a little bit more expressive and demonstrative as an African American male—I grew up in the neighborhood not too far from the neighborhood that feeds my school—so if I have to be a little more expressive in my communications because that's the norm in my neighborhood," then I need to be able to display that for my students, he said. "First, they're able to see that communication style as a positive, and they're able to incorporate that in" their own communications, but perhaps most importantly, it leads to an ability to recognize the difference between when a child is truly exhibiting aggressive behavior versus when a child is just communicating in a way that is common to his or her environment.

"And then we can have a conversation around behavior and discipline, and then there are teachers that understand when students do a certain thing it's not an aggressive action, it's not disrespectful, it's around communication style, it's also around certain norms in the neighborhood," he said. And we can begin "dissecting some of the referrals," asking teachers "what do you mean by disrespect, and are we imposing some of our middle-class norms on these students? There's a normalizing process," he said.

A 2014 report from the American Psychological Association found people—including police—saw Black boys as young as 10 "may not be viewed in the same light of childhood innocence as their white peers, but are instead more likely to be mistaken as older, be perceived as guilty and face police violence if accused of a crime" (Goff, Jackson, Di Leone, Culotta, & DiTomasso, 2014). A similar study from Georgetown University law school's Center on Poverty and Inequality found Black girls as young as five experience "adultfication" and are not afforded the same presumption of innocence as White girls (Epstein, Blake, & Gonzalez, 2017).

"There's a fear of our boys and our girls," said Turner, "and so because they don't understand and because they fear, there's this need for control and there's this power struggle that takes place."

Turner said he's worked with his staff to implement restorative discipline and cultural proficiency modules— "just to have a better understanding of our own biases and how they impact our interaction with our kids."

"Nationally, the narrative on Charlotte is that we are experiencing the fleecing of the urban district and the re-segregation because of the charter school movement," he said, "but if we were performing better in the traditional public schools, then the charters wouldn't be so appealing to families."

REFERENCES

Chetty, R., Hendren, N., Kline, P., & Saez, P. (2014). Where is the land of opportunity? The geography of intergenerational mobility in the United States. *The Quarterly Journal of Economics, 129*(4), 1553–1623.

Epstein, R., Blake, J., & Gonzalez, T. (2017). Girlhood interrupted: The erasure of Black girls' childhood. *SSRN Electronic Journal*.doi:10.2139/ssrn.3000695

Helms, A.D. (2017, February 1). Why CMS data on race and suspensions could shape talks about wherekids go to school. *The Charlotte Observer*. Retrieved from http://www.charlotte.com

Goff, P. A., Jackson, M. C., Di Leone, B. A. L., Culotta, C. M., & DiTomasso, N. A. (2014, February 24). The essence of innocence: Consequences of dehumanizing outgroup children. *Journal of Personality and Social Psychology*. Retrieved from http://www.apa.org/pubs/journals/releases/psp-a0035663.pdf

Oral History Interview with Arthur Griffin. (1999, May 7). Interview K-0168. Southern Oral History Program Collection (#4007) in the Southern Oral History Program Collection, Southern Historical Collection, Wilson Library, University of North Carolina at Chapel Hill.

Oyler, M. (2018, February 5). New developments in historically Black neighborhoods: New mixed-use may rebuild charlotte's second ward, but it's no replacement. *BisNow*. Retrieved from https://www.bisnow.com/charlotte/news/neighborhood/will-a-new-mixed-use-development-ease-the-pain-of-second-wards-past-84490

CHAPTER 5

CHICAGO

INTRODUCTION

As a community organizer and Southside resident, I have witnessed the shift in communities in this city through neighborhood revitalization efforts for close to 25 years. This revitalization often involves the removal of low- to middle-income people, as well as the closing of community schools. When I first moved to Chicago, I lived in Bronzeville, a traditionally African American area on the city's Southeast side, nestled between the Dan Ryan Expressway and Lake Michigan. I could walk to 31st Street Beach in under 15 minutes. I could get downtown in about the same time.

Just a few blocks west of me were the Robert Taylor Homes where my siblings were raised before our exodus to the suburbs. As children, my siblings attended Beethoven Elementary School, which was located on 47th and State Streets. Over the years I have seen the destruction and removal of public housing through an initiative called the Chicago Housing Authority's Plan for Transformation, launched by then-Mayor Richard M. Daley in 2000. Daley called it "the largest, most ambitious redevelopment of public housing in the United States" (Dumke, 2017). Four years after the CHA transformation, Mayor Richard Daley also launched a plan called Renaissance 2010, which was a plan to close 80 failing neighborhood schools and open 100 new charter schools by 2010. The new schools would be governed in structure as performance, charter and contract.

Let's Stop Calling It an Achievement Gap, pp. 47–58
Copyright © 2019 by Information Age Publishing
All rights of reproduction in any form reserved.

Many of the schools that were closed were located in predominantly Black and brown communities. But data show the Renaissance, architected and taken to a national level by Arne Duncan, largely failed our students and our communities. Displaced students were mostly shifted to other low-performing schools (Banchero, Germuska, & Little, 2010), and many of the displaced teachers were not given the opportunity to work in the new schools (Stokes, 2016). From 2000 to present Chicago has lost close to 200,000 Black residents because of the lack of housing choices and schooling options. Low enrollment has been used to justify many of the school closures.

Community-based schools have often been viewed as assets and a place to build strong and cohesive networks. The buildings have served as places where children and adults alike could be educated—many adults received GED training at the schools after hours. The playgrounds were a safe space for young people to develop their athletic skills and play close to home. Some neighborhood schools have seen generations of the same families, and when you close these schools, you tear away at the basic fabric of social networks. When young people are forced to leave the schools they have been accustomed to, data tells us that the student will regress academically. One of the many failures of Renaissance 2010 is that it did not track the students who were displaced, it did not offer additional counseling and it did not offer additional academic support. However, the schools which retained the same students, building a network of support around them rather than forcing them to relocate under new leadership, saw those students progress academically (Banchero, Germuska, & Little, 2010).

Many of the young people who I have mentored had school days that would begin with a 6:00 A.M. commute and end at 6:00 P.M. Students and their parents would often talk about the lack of local choices for a quality education. According to data, in Illinois per pupil spending ranges from $32,000 in some districts to $5,000 in other districts (Cunningham, 2018). Part of this is due to an antiquated education funding formula that was based on property taxes. Due to decades of systemic racism, redlining, divestment and crime, housing values on the south and west sides of the city have not grown at the rate of other property values around the city. Therefore, many schools lacked proper support and investment.

The lack of investment put many of our children in harm's way. Because of the changes brought about by Renaissance 2010, children were enrolled in schools where the schools they left were traditional rivals with the new schools they entered. There should have been integration plans which considered the social constructs in place in the city. Due to the lack of planning, our children were placed in harm's way, and in the most disastrous cases lost their lives attempting to navigate gang territories to attend schools that had overcrowded classrooms and were disproportionately underresourced.

Currently, there are Safe Passage programs that employ community residents to watch young people navigate certain communities.

Due to the implementation of Zero Tolerance Policies in Chicago Public Schools (CPS), our schools have been placed on a direct pipeline to the prison industrial complex. There is ample research that talks about the correlations between third grade test scores and entry into prisons. Failed policies have failed our greatest asset. Our children have been moved, suspended, expelled, arrested, pushed out, kicked out and denied an equitable and fruitful educational experience.

As a Chicago resident, I am proud to know of the parents and community-based organizations who were willing to lead hunger strikes and sit-ins to combat school closings, legislators who created legislation to take booking stations out of schools, the Chicago Teachers Union who pushed back against the city, and the many educators who have used their own resources to clothe, feed and provide school supplies for countless children. They represent the sunlight in a dark place. They represent possibility and hope for our children and communities.

Bryan Echols, MA, is a community organizer and activist in Chicago, who is particularly passionate about improving outcomes for Black men in the city.

CHICAGO

Extreme Decentralization and an Investment in Principals

In November of 1987, then-U.S. Secretary of Education William Bennett called Chicago Public Schools the worst school system in America. A 43% dropout rate and dismal scores on the American College Test led Bennett to encourage leaders to "explode the blob," create a school-based accountability system and increase school choice efforts in the district (Banas & Byers, 1987). The comments were particularly offensive to Chicagoans given that his boss, President Ronald Reagan, had significantly stripped education funding and was largely blamed for the dismantling of public education across the country (Verstegen, 1990).

What would result, via state legislation passed the following year and an amendment that would follow in 1995, would be a comprehensive reform effort that has led to what is today the most decentralized of any of the large public school districts in the country, giving control of the city's schools to locally elected school councils for each building, rather than to a central office ("Reform Before the Storm," 2012).

The district has seen no shortage of teacher strikes and budget woes in the decades followed. Roughly one-third of students in Chicago live in poverty, and African American children in particular are twice as impacted by poverty as others in the city (Ihejirika, 2015). Former Chicago Public Schools Chief Education Officer Forrest Claypool said there are still "two separate but unequal funding systems" in the city, which he said is "partially based on how the state funds teacher retirements and pensions"—Chicago is the only district in the state that has to pay its own, and cash deficits in the district correlate directly with the pension obligations, he said during a July 2017 meeting in his office. Claypool believes the disparities are a result of "really strong racial overtones" in a system that gives schools which are heavily populated by African American students "only a fraction of the funding that white, more affluent students receive."

"There is no other place in the United States where the state itself deliberately provides hundreds of millions of dollars less funding to African American and Latino children," he said, calling it "straightforward discrimination" against students of color. "This is not about adequacy," he said, pointing out that Chicago enrolls roughly 20% of the state's total population of students, but receives only 15% of state funding when you include teacher pension funding. "It's about racially-based unequal funding—60 years after *Brown*."

"Separate is never equal when it comes to education funding and race, especially here in Illinois ... the land of Lincoln and the land of Barack Obama, ironically," said Claypool, who would leave his post in the district following an ethics probe just a few months later. That separation permeates through, even stems from, a long history of racial discrimination in housing and zoning practices in the city, a fact which remains true in many cities across the country, using a model which many say was perfected in Chicago (Moser, 2015).

The Turnaround

Chicago's current Chief Education Officer, Janice Jackson, was in fifth grade at John W. Cook Elementary School in the city's Auburn Gresham neighborhood when Bill Bennett called her system the worst in the nation. As someone who started in Chicago Public Schools in Head Start, graduated from Hyde Park High School and would complete all of her education at public institutions in the state of Illinois, this statement was deeply personal for Jackson.

And she's inherited the reins of the district at a great time. Chicago is being heralded as a national example for urban turnaround. It is considered one of the highest-performing districts in the country and is enjoying improved graduation rates, improved on-track rates, and improvement in standardized test rates. In third grade, students start out about the same as students in other districts, but in the 5 years to eighth grade, they've been able to get 6 years of learning, Jackson said. And most importantly, she said, the "reforms work for all students," forcing a need for "an important acknowledgement around what African American and Latino students can do."

She acknowledges there's a long way to go—despite the fact that progress has been continuous and steady for all groups in the last 5 to 10 years, gaps persist around racial and socioeconomic lines. Jackson said she is particularly driven by bridging the system's opportunity gap and making sure students of color have the same opportunities, and same access to international baccalaureate and advanced placement courses, as others in the city.

"What does give me hope is that when you do an apples to apples comparison to their peers across the state, on every demographic indicator [CPS students are], outperforming their peers in the state. All tides are rising, but we know that we started with that gap" and there's still a ways to go to close it, she said.

She said the district is taking a "multi-pronged approach," to control the things it can control, like striving to have 50% of students finish high school with some kind of postsecondary credential, whether with AP or IB credit, early or dual enrollment credit. Mayor Rahm Emanuel controversially implemented a requirement that all CPS students furnish either a college acceptance letter or a job offer to receive their high school diploma (Byrne, Perez, & Dardick, 2017)—a policy which received heavy criticism from parties across the country, despite the fact that all CPS graduates are guaranteed admission to the City Colleges of Chicago community college system.

The move was intended to get students thinking about their futures, the mayor said, which is something a lot of students in the system may be missing, according to Jackson, who said her own goals to make sure students finish high school with some college credit "makes our students feel like they're college material, gives them confidence—with a lot of our students, they may be academically ready, but they don't have the confidence or the financial support."

Focusing on Leadership

A focus on investing in principal development and evaluating the changing role of principals in the district have been integral to the rising tides of student achievement. With so many schools in what is the nation's third-largest district, "the thinking is it's much easier to control for the work of having good administrators in the building" and empowering them to lead, Jackson said in July 2017 meeting.

So the district has partnered with the Chicago Public Education fund and other community partners to focus on principal support, retention and development. Because of the 1988 and 1995 reforms, principal hiring is handled by the local school councils—which are comprised of teachers, parents, and community members from that school. Jackson said "the principals have been a key lever of change in Chicago. I think leadership matters, and there's been a lot of turnover at the CEO level,"—12 chief education officers in fewer than 28 years—and Jackson said the district would not have been able to realize growth "if not for great leadership at the school level."

With the partnership of the fund—an independent local nonprofit run by community members with a vested interest in the success of Chicago's public education—CPS focuses heavily on principal training, which includes some advocacy work and exposure to policy, as well as supports for the budget-making process—which is entirely determined by the principals themselves and approved by their school councils. Schools are given a lump-sum budget based on enrollment, but it is up to local principals to determine how those funds will be spent, and local school councils to approve those plans.

Jackson is particularly proud that principals who are selected as fellows in a leadership program supported by the fund "do policy work." She said the most transformative advice she received as a principal was to not "complain about policy, because policy can be changed in 45 days." As a district leader, she has sought to bring that to scale by empowering other principals, through a fellowship program supported by the fund, to get some political experience. Not only does this give the district 30–40 principals per year who can be "out on the front lines advocating for the things that matter," it also gives these principals a better understanding of what district administrators are faced with and helps them better understand budget allocations and reduce complaints.

After accounting for legacy debt and pension obligations, the amount of money that actually makes it to schools is pretty small, and leaders realized they could either chart out one path that they hoped would work for all of the schools, or they could allow principals to make decisions on the ground.

"I think that's a real decision point for all public school systems, and I think that's where Chicago has made a different choice," said Heather Anichini, president and CEO of the Chicago Public Education Fund.

Rodolfo Rojas, principal of Edward Everett Elementary School, participated in the program and said the opportunity really gave him an appreciation for "how limited the money is and how far they have to stretch it." But decentralizing budget decisions also allows individual school leaders to make decisions, even regarding scarce resources, that will have the most impact on the ground for their student populations.

At Everett Elementary, where 95% of students receive free and reduced lunch, and close to 50% are English Language Learners, this means Rojas can make the call to put additional support in the classroom, providing an assistant for nearly every teacher to make sure "we're hitting every student, every day."

But filling teacher positions has been a continual challenge given the state's budget woes he said, particularly in specialized areas like special education or bilingual education. The budget was rolling out so late that a lot of the teachers have already rolled out to other districts" by the time he could even post positions. There's been some improvement; in 2018 some budget stability has arisen allowing him to post positions earlier.

As part of the concerted effort to focus on principals, the district has focused heavily on the idea that the principal's job is "not just about discipline and order, but it's about being the chief academic learning officer" in the school, responsible for both student and teacher learning. The autonomy afforded to principals, Jackson believes, helps to attract high-quality people to the job.

Rojas was also a student in CPS and said he finds the work of "affecting students like myself ... very satisfying." He also said he finds the support of the district and the fund critical, ensuring he is better prepared by helping him to work on better relationships with teachers in the building.

Increasing Accountability and Transparency

But greater autonomy can't come without greater accountability, and according to Jackson, the district's accountability system prioritizes growth and takes into consideration things like students being on track and incentives for growth.

Key to this idea is an emphasis on transparency to all stakeholders, and at the center of this transparency movement is a partnership with the University of Chicago's Urban Education Institute, which provides student and school-level data—before the district has had a chance to review it—to the university, which then provides feedback to the local principals that they can use to enact real-time change.

One of the biggest metrics to come of this partnership is the idea of "freshmen on track," which refutes conventional knowledge about the importance of pre-high school factors on a student's likelihood to be prepared for and attend college. The freshman on track metric said that a student's performance in his or her freshman year of high school is one of the biggest indicators of whether they will be college-ready. Leaders in CPS say this data has revolutionized the way teachers in the school teach, because, as Sara Ray Stoelinga, director of the Urban Education Institute at the University of Chicago, said, "it went against strongly held beliefs about what matters for high school graduation—there were some thoughts that it was test scores, some thought that by high school, it was too late," so a realization that high school could make a difference changed the approach to the job for many teachers.

Stoelinga said the institute remains "policy-neutral," and doesn't make recommendations to the district or the mayor's office on how schools should act on the information provided, which she believes is very important to the relationship. Instead, reports are generated every 6 weeks, which gives school leaders a chance to evaluate and implement changes for specific students while it still matters. "What we're doing is trying to sort of hold up the data to the district in a way that said 'here is what your data say' but not offering any solid solution," she said, which is important to the overall idea of principal autonomy in the district.

"This idea of linking K–12 kids with their higher education results [before they even get there] is something that had never been done before," she said. "I think making this link helped people to really look forward to the horizon and say 'we are responsible for our young people's trajectories after they leave here.'"

"What's important to us is that we are trying out things in our school system, but it's grounded in research from the university," said Jackson. "There's also this trusting relationship that allows us to give them access and for them to be completely honest with us.... I remember being a principal and hearing about this [freshman on track] metric, and thinking 'wow, students are much more likely to graduate if they're on track by the end of the freshman year,' and principals around the country really started to energize around that."

But this kind of partnership is one that turns a lot of leaders off. Jackson said the first key to the success of a partnership like this is embracing the idea that you have to turn over data on teacher and student performance without analyzing it or cleaning it up first. This increases accountability because all stakeholders have access to the information, said Jackson, who believes Chicago Public Schools' "level of accountability is great."

"We track almost everything and it's posted and available for review and debate," she said, noting that she likes the transparency, because not only does it hold officials accountable to the population they're serving, it makes external partners more willing to work with the district. Anichini said other districts looking to attract community support should "pick a perspective around which all of the work centers around," whether that's leadership or teachers, and "make sure you keep an eye on how policy is affecting people on the ground."

Moving to Scale

In every city, resources are scarce, but mobilizing around common issues is the surest way to effect measurable change, she said. And Jackson adds the importance of making sure the school quality policies align with the articulated goals—if you say you're serious about equity in education, it should be written down as one of the policy tenants, she said.

And, said Stoelinga, "data is not enough. You have to have research, data, and professional learning before people can do anything with it. Unless you have this combination of research-based understanding and data in your hands at the right time, in the right format coupled with this professional learning," it will not work, she said.

Jackson said the model works in Chicago, because of its size and a realization that "innovation moves faster on the ground," but second because of the leadership of not just school principals, but parents, local school councils and strong leadership across the board, which enables "a faster impact."

"The most scarce resource is time, not money, and giving leaders and educators time to meet and process info is most critical," Stoelinga said.

REFERENCES

Banas, C., & Byers, D. (1987, November 8). Education chief: City schools worst. *Chicago Tribune*. Retrieved from https://www.chicagotribune.com/news/ct-xpm-1987-11-08-8703230953-story.html

Banchero, S., Germuska, J., & Little, D. (2010, January 17). Daley school plan fails to make grade. *Chicago Tribune*. Retrieved from http://articles.chicagotribune.com/2010-01-17/news/1001160276_1_charter-schools-chicago-reform-urban-education

Byrne, J., Perez, J., Jr., & Dardick, H. (2017, April 5). Emanuel wants to add a CPS graduation requirement: Get acceptance letter. *Chicago Tribune*. Retrieved from http://www.chicagotribune.com/news/local/politics/ct-rahm-emanuel-high-school-requirement-met-20170405-story.html

Cunningham, P. (2018, January 16). What's driving chicago's school turnaround success? Lessons from 30 years of ed reform [Editorial]. *The 74*. Retrieved from https://www.the74million.org/article/cunningham-whats-driving-chicagos-school-turnaround-success-lessons-from-30-years-of-ed-reform/

Dumke, M. (2017, September 3). Years late, with big gaps, CHA nears end of housing 'transformation'. *Chicago Sun-Times*. Retrieved from https://chicago.suntimes.com/feature/years-late-with-big-gaps-cha-nears-end-of-housing-transformation/

Ihejirika, M. (2015, July 22). More children in Illinois, U.S. living in poverty than before recession. *Chicago Sun-Times*. Retrieved from https://chicago.suntimes.com/chicago-politics/more-children-in-illinois-u-s-living-in-poverty-than-before-recession/

Moser, W. (2014, May 5). Housing discrimination in America was perfected in Chicago. *Chicago Magazine*. Retrieved from http://www.chicagomag.com/city-life/May-2014/The-Long-Shadow-of-Housing-Discrimination-in-Chicago/

Reform before the storm: A timeline of the Chicago public schools. (2012, October 2). *Chicago Magazine*. Retrieved from http://www.chicagomag.com/Chicago-Magazine/November-2012/Reform-Before-the-Storm-Chicago-Public-Schools-Timeline/

Stokes, D. (2016). *The limits of education reform in New Orleans and Chicago* (Working paper). Annandale-on-Hudson, NY: Bard College. Retrieved from https://digitalcommons.bard.edu/cgi/viewcontent.cgi?article=1243&context=senproj_s2016.

Verstegen, D. (Winter 1990). Education fiscal policy in the Reagan administration. *Educational Evaluation and Policy Analysis, 12*(4), 355–373.

CHAPTER 6

DALLAS

INTRODUCTION

His Name is Today

"We are guilty of many errors and many
faults,
But our worst crime is abandoning the
children,
Neglecting the fountain of life.
Many of the things we need can wait,
The child cannot wait.
Right now is the time his bones are being
formed,
His blood is being made,
And his senses are being developed.
To him we cannot answer 'tomorrow'
His name is Today.

—Gabriela Mistral

In one of my favorite movies, *To Sir With Love*, Sidney Poitier stars in the title role as a secondary school teacher in a downtrodden area of London. He is an engineer by training who, as a result of his inability to find employment in his field, accepts a teaching position in a neighborhood school that bears an uncanny situational resemblance to those one finds in the neglected parts of Chicago, Baltimore, and Dallas. Poitier quickly realizes that lesson planning and standardized test scores mean little in a world where managing the day-to-day reality of scarcity takes precedence over everything else, including academic achievement.

When I was younger, part of the reason *To Sir With Love* stood out to me was because it was so different from what I personally experienced. So much so, that I thought theirs was an outlier scenario. However, what my career in education has taught me is that unfortunately, students living with the ravages of poverty is not the outlier. Sadly, it has become the norm in this country. The truth of the matter is that America is now a country whose educational system is defined by poverty —the majority of students in public K–12 education now qualify for free and reduced lunch plans and 54% of all college students are utilizing Pell Grants to pay for their schooling ("A New Majority," 2015).

In Dallas, one does not need to look very far to understand what students living in poverty looks like. Dallas Independent School District (DISD) classifies 86.1% of all of its students as economically disadvantaged (Enrollment Statistics, n.d.). This means that Dallas has a public school system where all but a select few of its students come from families that are faced with the type of lives where academics are often a secondary concern.

For many people, such a trade-off between life and learning would seem unimaginable. However, those people most likely do not live under the specter of homelessness, food insecurity, unemployment, underemployment, poor healthcare, and/or a lack of safety. Students raised in these types of environments are more at risk for academic and social problems, poor health and a life filled with economic hardships (Engle & Black, 2008). The only way that these students can consistently persevere is by establishing support systems that are capable of mitigating the harmful effects of poverty.

Designing a model that will be effective requires more than just addressing the role that poverty plays. It also requires acknowledging the role that race plays in DISD. DISD is a school district where only 4% of its students identify as White. This means that essentially DISD is a school district for Black and brown kids whose families live in poverty. This composition of the school district has frustrated elected officials, teachers, and administrators for decades. It has also colored the expectations that far too many people in this city have for the life outcomes of these students and the futures of the communities that produce them.

Dallas and most of our nation's school systems do not yet adequately address the realities of life spent in schools segregated by race and class. By not doing so, our schools fail to unlock the full potential of our children. The results of this failure are school districts and cities with the diminishing opportunity to end the cycle of poverty that strangle so many promising minds.

At Paul Quinn College, we believe that we have created the model for how schools can address the needs of students from underresourced backgrounds while simultaneously providing them a pathway out of poverty. In addition to providing every student with much-needed wraparound services, we also now provide them with jobs via our Urban Work College Model. By doing so, we believe we have created a level playing field that allows our students' true abilities to shine.

Demographically, Paul Quinn's student body is similar to that of DISD. Annually, 80–90% of the college's students are Pell Grant eligible and 98% of them are either Black or Hispanic. Additionally, 70% of PQC students are members of families where no one has the means to contribute monetarily to the cost of a college education. The only real differences between Paul Quinn's students and DISD's population are age and the fact that 40% of the college's students come from outside the state of Texas. The fact that Paul Quinn's model works with the same type of students, at the college level, is proof that it has the ability to go beyond the confines of higher education.

Education doesn't end poverty. Jobs end poverty. Wealth ends poverty. A life that lends itself to the ability to access the opportunities that one's talents afford them ends poverty. Poverty defines and will continue to define public education in this city until we face its ravages head-on. We must acknowledge that only focusing on what happens during the school day without addressing the impact of one's total economic circumstance is a strategy that produces only fool's gold and work harder to improve the conditions around our students to promote greater success overall.

Michael J. Sorrell, EdD, is president of Paul Quinn College, which was founded in 1872 to educate freed slaves and their offspring. Kerry L. Condon serves as special assistant to the president.

DALLAS

All Hands on Deck to Ensure Smoother Hand-Offs Between Schools and the Workforce

In the late 1950s, the founders of Texas Instruments, Inc. found themselves frustrated by a dearth of qualified individuals in the Dallas-Ft. Worth area who had advanced training in engineering and the physical sciences; the universities in the region were simply not turning out enough graduates in these fields to meet the company's demand, and Texas Instruments was having to recruit from outside of the state to close the gaps.

"You have this tale of two cities" in Dallas, said Dallas County Community College District Chancellor Joe May. On the one hand, there's a city which is benefiting from "a booming economy with incredible economic growth with jobs being created—literally 335 jobs a day being created. But on the other hand, there's a city which has the highest child poverty rate in the country and sees a great portion of its population being boxed out of that economic vitality."

With this in mind, the founders of Texas Instruments took it upon themselves to launch what is now the University of Texas at Dallas to help bridge that gap. But "you soon realize that if you want to change the equation there [at the university level], you have to back up into high school, and if you want to change the equation there, you have to back up into middle school, and on and on," said former math teacher and current Texas Instruments President of Ed Tech division and leader of the company's academic engagement and corporate citizenship, Peter Balyta. "Just writing a check doesn't help. Sometimes it makes the problem worse. We needed very tangible, hands-on engagement to help steer" the preparedness of the company's future STEM workforce.

Today, Texas Instruments joins more than 50 partners from tech and business in Dallas—"from a Who's Who of corporations in Dallas to small companies," according to Dallas Independent School District Superintendent Michael Hinojosa, who are joining forces with the district and local colleges to ensure today's students are prepared to succeed in tomorrow's workforce.

"The mayor keeps talking about there's all these jobs that go unfulfilled in Dallas, and that's because" the schools weren't preparing the students to meet the demands, Hinojosa said. As such, the formation of many of the partnerships, much like the creation of UT Dallas, have been largely driven by the companies which call the Dallas-Ft. Worth area home.

"This has been beyond my wildest dreams how successful this has become, and we kind of stumbled into it," said Hinojosa of the partnerships unfolding between the district, industry and local colleges and universities. "I've never seen anything like it in my 23 years as superintendent, the way this came together."

For example, he said, the college academies, or P-Techs as they're called, were born out of an idea pitched by executives from American Airlines, which is headquartered in Dallas, who "were very frustrated they were having to go all over the world to hire a diverse workforce."

One of the executives "came to us and asked if he could lease one of our buildings ... to start a training program for 19, 20, 21 year-olds" to teach them the skills needed to work at the company, Hinojosa said. The district ultimately decided they wanted to be involved in the efforts, but since they don't serve 19–21 year-olds, they knew they'd need some help from the local community college district.

Hinojosa recalled that "May said we always mess up in the hand-off," said Hinojosa, "so what these collegiate academies, these P-Techs, have done is minimize the opportunities to fumble the hand-off."

"Every time we remove friction between systems, it increases the likelihood that people will be successful," said May. "Most people aren't lost or drop out because of the content; they drop off because of poor hand-offs in the system and a lack of clarity about what needs to happen."

So, said May, what the system is trying to do is figure out "how to identify friction, how to identify barriers that are getting in the way." Part of this he sees as being tied into the partnership with Dallas ISD, but it's more than that. "We're bringing in private philanthropy, we're bringing in transportation [partnerships] and we're bringing in food, we're continuing to look at this" holistically, said May, who detailed partnerships between the community college district and the city's public transit system and local food pantries to care for students' total needs.

"We've now partnered with DART … where we purchase public transportation passes for any student [enrolled] half-time or more [to be able to get around] not just to school, but to anywhere. We've continued that, realizing that while in high school, many students were receiving meals, but when they come to college, that's not something we provide," May said, adding they've worked on "bringing mobile food pantries to our campus as well."

Leveling the Playing Field

University of North Texas at Dallas President Bob Mong said his institution signed on as the only four-year partner, joining the Dallas County Community College District to invest in the pipeline because "if you look at it from a national perspective and you look at a few years ago, lines crossed and a majority of public school students are [now] eligible for free or reduced lunch. That's a pretty seismic difference … so we felt at our school that we should really focus on that population that received free and reduced lunch. That was our mission," said May, who adds that the university was originally established in Southern Dallas by the legislators "to serve a historically underserved area."

"We want to get better and better at serving those students," he said. "Our strategic initiative is really for the university to be a pathway of social mobility for our students, … because most of our students come from the bottom economic third or below … most of them are first-generation students. And so the [Dallas Independent School District] covers much of our tier one recruitment area."

One of the things about the multi-tiered partnership which stands out is it places competitive, sought-after programs in schools and neighborhoods which would traditionally be overlooked in other places.

"We've got kids going to tough neighborhoods and they're not afraid, because they've got something great going for them," said Hinojosa.

In other places around the country, top students from "bad" neighborhoods and schools would be bussed out to top programs, which means there is no success modeling for students who aren't seen as top students, and there is a reinforcement of the deficit narrative these students face daily. In Dallas, however, the message is clear: All students in all neighborhoods deserve access to quality schools.

"We've always had competition from private schools, and the big challenge is charter schools are recruiting our kids, and if you don't give them something they want, you're going to lose them," said Hinojosa.

As an added benefit for the schools, "American Airlines decided to put their own equipment into El Centro [College, one of the partnering community colleges], to train" students on the technology they'd actually be using in the field.

And the entrance criteria for the career academies isn't based on test scores, but interviews. The main thing school leaders are looking to ascertain: "Do you want this, or does your mom want this" for you?

"We don't cream the best students," said May, emphasizing the idea that the early college and P-Tech programs are open to all who want the chance to enter.

For a population of "mostly first-generation, 90% economically disadvantaged students," the most important thing is to provide an opportunity for the students to better themselves, but it has to be one they're willing to work for themselves.

"You get smarter through hard work, you learn how to develop resiliency through grit," Hinojosa said.

However, once students make that decision, they're set on a pathway which increases their chances of success exponentially.

"The student, the moment they decide to go into high school in the 9th grade, they decide to go to college, it's not a separate decision," said May.

"The partnership really happens coming out of the eighth grade. We work with them on the curriculum, we work on a minimum of two business partners that would go into the schools, our faculty get engaged, he said. In 9th grade, there is a heightened focus on reading. In 10th, it's writing, and in 11th, it's mathematics, said May, who described "incredible gains" from this approach, and boasted "97–100% students staying in the program, a 93%-plus graduation rate out of students who quite frankly wouldn't have been predicted to be that high, and they're 100% college ready."

Making It Official

Hinojosa said the biggest hindrance for districts looking to arrange similar types of partnerships is a lack of infrastructure.

"We'll ask people to come in and do stuff, and they'll show up and we'll have them make copies and get coffee for people, and that's not really engagement," he said.

"In the past," arrangements were "haphazard and one-off," Hinojosa continued. In some cases, "someone adopted a school, and that was great," he said. But there was no follow through.

"The beautiful thing about this is it's not just a pat on the back or a 'come when you can' or a 'we'd like you to help'—there's actually a memorandum of understanding that lines out what everyone is supposed to do, when they're supposed to come," he said. "There's a place for everybody."

"It's laid out in a very organized way all over the district," he said. "Each one of [the partnerships] is unique, but there's been a niche" each has been able to fill. "Every school has a staff member who's assigned to make sure they take care of those industry partners," he said.

And that staffer is an assistant principal-level official whose primary job is managing relationships, not a junior level person or someone who is splitting time between numerous functions.

"By putting some infrastructure and support in it, it'll help us stay true to the design and the process" and get actual results, Hinojosa said.

Putting Students First

May and Mong both emphasized their dedication to working with the students who come out of Dallas ISD, whether or not those students ever end up on one of their respective campuses.

"Part of it is just letting the principals and educators and counselors know that we care about their students. Not enough of them go to college—that's well-documented," said Mong. "From their coming their freshman year, we're involved. We're on the advisory boards."

"The idea is that these young people would graduate with an associate degree and then they could go on ... obviously, we'd like some of those kids to go here, but ... anything that gets kids going to college more, being better positioned for the future, regardless of where they go" is a win for the whole region, Mong said. "They don't have to come here, they could go somewhere else, but our feeling was that it was an important partnership for us to be involved, whether they end up coming here or not."

May agreed, saying, "What we realized is if we really put the student at the center of what we're doing—if we really care about their needs, we really need to put the students first, not the needs of the college first, at the expense of the student."

"As we look at success, we're also really focusing on understanding that many of the students are coming to us, we may be the closest college to them, but we may not be the best college for them," May said.

And so, at the Dallas County Community College District, the idea was to put in place navigators which are "institution agnostic" to "help get the student from where they are to where they need to be," regardless of where that is, he said.

"We had many, many students that were going to multiple colleges at the same time. What was really interesting about those students is they tended to be very successful. They tended to have good grade point averages, they tended to graduate, they tended to be very successful when they transferred," he said. And ultimately, the success of those students is the success of the entire region.

As such, the Dallas County Community College District provides scholarships to cover the full cost for the students in the early high school programs, including the cost of course materials, and the cost for those who don't finish their associate degrees alongside their high school diplomas, either because they weren't enrolled in a participating school or because they didn't have all of the credits needed, which May said equals about two-thirds of students in the district.

The Dallas County Promise program, which Mong said is modeled after the Tennessee Promise program and which UNT Dallas was instrumental in helping to push, despite being a four-year institution, "promises any student, not just the early college students, but any student the opportunity to continue their education for free," May said.

As long as students "commit to college by January of their senior year, complete the FAFSA by March of their senior year, and meet with our mentor-coaches during that senior year, and if they do those three things, we will provide scholarship funds to cover the remaining cost of whatever isn't covered," May said.

Mong said beyond institutional mission, the main impetus for the university to intervene on behalf of students who may not ultimately choose to attend UNT Dallas is alignment with the state coordinating board's 60-30 goal—a benchmark which seeks to get "60% of 25–34 year olds by 2030 to have at least a credential or a bachelor's degree or associate's degree"—and it will take a comprehensive effort from every school in the state to get there.

REFERENCES

A new majority: Low income students now a majority in the nation's public schools. (2015, January). Retrieved from http://www.southerneducation.org/getattachment/4ac62e27-5260-47a5-9d02-14896ec3a531/A-New-Majority-2015-Update-Low-Income-Students-Now.aspx

Engle, P. L., & Black, M. W. (2008, July 25). The effect of poverty on child development and educational outcomes. *The New York Academy of Sciences*. https://doi.org/10.1196/annals.1425.023

Enrollment Statistics (as of 06/01/2018). (n.d.). Retrieved from https://mydata.dallasisd.org/SL/SD/ENROLLMENT/Enrollment.jsp?SLN=1000

CHAPTER 7

HOUSTON

INTRODUCTION

The landmark ruling of *Brown v. Board of Education* was one of the most influential rulings decisively affecting how the African American community would engage with schools. The ruling validated the notion that "in the field of public education, the doctrine of 'separate but equal' has no place. Separate educational facilities are inherently unequal" (Klineberg, 2018). The turning point meant Black children would hopefully be allowed to fully participate in the promise of education that had solely been the right of White children.

Sixty-five years later, we continue to see the ruling from the Supreme Court was not realized in our educational system. The nation has not lived up to the promises the African American community believed would manifest once separate but equal was determined to be inherently unequal. More specifically, I believe in 2018, we continue to witness the aftermath of broken promises from our policymakers, legislators, and the educational community. The children are the victim of a society and system that has never fully appreciated or valued the role of the African American learner, and the gaps are evidence our crimes and broken commitments to serve the children in our care. As with the nation, this is also the case in Houston, Texas.

Let's Stop Calling It an Achievement Gap, pp. 71–79
Copyright © 2019 by Information Age Publishing
All rights of reproduction in any form reserved.

Instead of blaming the victim, it is time to begin transforming the mind-sets and the pedagogy around educating this population so that success is a priority. My own transformation began when I started to critically reflect on my career as an educator. As a young teacher, working in a predomi-nately Black and Hispanic community, I should have studied and taken more risks to ensure each of my students (and their families) had access to the promises education offered. As an administrator, I should have worked harder to hold my teachers accountable for the success of each student and the community at large.

Now, my current role in higher education allows me to create spaces where educators can learn about the process of internal and external change in order to support each child on their campus, but specifically the unique needs of those who have been historically marginalized. My service to the profession through communities like Advancing Issues Regarding Race and Equity (AIRRE) fuels my passion to give back and help others gain the skills necessary to lead using equity frameworks. As time passes, I gain more understanding of what it takes to become an influential educa-tor and leader.

Houston can definitely become the leader in realizing what equity in education can achieve. The School Reform Initiative (2018) defines educational equity as "the practice of ensuring that each child is success-ful regardless of their external or internal, social or cultural contexts" (para. 2). Using this definition as a lens, it is our duty as educators and leaders to confront any pedagogies and practices that prohibit some stu-dents from accessing the same educational opportunities as their peers (Gorski, 2015). Practically, this means engaging with other educators and leaders to do the *heart* work involved in changing mindsets, creating new paradigms, and restructuring systems to better support and educate Houston and surrounding communities. Through my story, I hope to inspire resilient and efficacious leaders willing to amplify the voices of the underserved as a means to create meaningful change through action.

Houston is a great training lab, because diversity abounds ethnically, racially, culturally, religiously, and linguistically in this rich city. According the U.S. Census (2017), Houston is the fourth largest city in the nation, and in 2016 the fastest growing. Within the city and surrounding areas, there will be differences between neighborhoods, school districts, and even schools within one district.

I am a proud Houstonian, because I believe our city can be a model for decreasing opportunity gaps across every grade level by creating an aware-ness of equity and supporting teachers in developing an equity pedagogy. Houston's diverse educational community needs to begin reframing how to address defunct educational practices in order to better support the critical learning needs of the African American student. I am also heartened by the recent discourse, locally and nationally, surrounding equity.

I look at the achievement gap and believe it is more a sign that teachers and leaders are not successfully teaching Black children in a way that is authentic, meaningful, and relevant. We have not given these children equitable opportunities to fully participate and thrive in the current system.

The willingness of many educators to engage in the uncomfortable conversations centering around the intersection of race and equity in schools is the first step in recognizing the problem that gains its roots in history. While the journey is ultimately one of personal transformation followed by professional action, I see many teachers willing to tackle the topic for children.

If we reframe our thinking to envision our educational system as a means to support children in obtaining the competencies to live a self-actualized life, then we would also spend more time addressing the oppressive systems that have yet to be confronted and are the root cause of apparent opportunity gaps in the first place. We would also hone the students' ability to critically think, question, and use their voices to create meaningful changes. Instead, we validate conformity, complicity, and silence as a way to navigate the system.

Desmond Tutu said, "I am not interested in picking up crumbs of compassion thrown from the table of someone who considers himself my master. I want the full menu of rights." Through my research and writing, I want to provide an insight to others about how urgent the need for equity is for Black children. By tapping into my platform, I am driven to help educators seeking justice for students to begin those critical conversations that will lead to awareness and action. I also want to be the catalyst for leaders to address systemic issues that restrict African American children from the opportunities of education and the ability to fully participate in the promises of education.

Kelly A. Brown, PhD, is an assistant professor of Educational Leadership in the Center for Doctoral Studies at Lamar University, whose research interests include examining policies and practices that have cultural implications for issues of equity in education. She previously served as a K–12 teacher and administrator in the city.

HOUSTON

Lost Economic Opportunities a Wake-Up Call to City Leaders

When Houston officials realized the city wasn't even a contender for Amazon's new headquarters, city leaders faced something of a wake-up call: Houston's poor education system would likely preclude it from any serious conversations about attracting new business to the area.

There's no zoning and very little public transportation in Houston. In 2010, a study profiled in the *Los Angeles Times* found the city had passed New York has the most diverse major metropolis in the nation (Mejia, 2017). There are over 100 languages spoken across Houston Independent School District, 12 with a critical enough mass of students to require services in those languages. Demographics experts call Houston a roadmap of what American cities will look like in the future, as non-White immigrant populations continue to increase and the White population decreases, forcing White residents to deal with being in the minority (Mejia, 2017).

The Houston Independent School District (HISD) supports over 215,000 students (HISD, 2018) and is the seventh largest school district in America ("Largest School Districts," n.d.). Black children make up roughly one-fourth of the district's population, but as is the case in many other major urban cities, they continue to lag behind every other ethnic subgroup in the city (Devries, 2017).

But research from Rice University's Kinder Institute has found that Black and Hispanic families place a consistently higher value on the importance of postsecondary education (Klineberg, 2018).

"If Houston's African American and Hispanic young people are not getting the education they need to succeed in today's economy, it is demonstrably not because they do not value that education or recognize its importance," the report reads. "It is because these two communities, which together represent fully 70 percent of all Harris County residents who are under the age of 20 today, are by far the most likely to be living in areas of concentrated disadvantage, with all that such poverty portends for a young person's ability to succeed in the public schools" (Klineberg, 2018).

Residents agree significantly more money needs to be spent on the city's schools (Klineberg, 2018)—presently, Houston Independent School District spends only $9,633 per student, an amount which, even after a 15% increase from 2015, still constitutes one of the lowest rates of state support for education among the nation's 50 largest school districts (LEAH). The district gets 74.3% of its revenue from local sources; the only district in the state which receives less funding from the state than Houston is Austin (Binkovitz, 2018). And as the state as a whole continues to try to rebound from steep cuts in 2011, a 2017 study from the University of Texas at Austin's UTeach Center found "in 2016 the lowest income elementary schools spent $256 less per student than in 2008 while the wealthiest elementary campuses spent $11 more" (Marder & Villanueva, 2017).

Even though Houston, under the leadership of a Black mayor and exemplifying attitudes which are much more favorable towards immigration and themes of diversity than other places in the state and around the country, shuns some of the more conservative politics of the state, Lanier Middle School Principal Katharine Bradarich said Texas' largest school district still has "a lot of distraction from the work of school mixed in the zeitgeist of Texas" politics. Some say Houston and Austin are being punished by Governor Greg Abbott for their liberal policies, particularly around immigration and their stances as "sanctuary cities" (Mejia, 2017). And, after district officials missed the deadline to submit a plan to turnaround its 10 failing schools, the district is facing a takeover by the state's education agency. Meaning the political zeitgeist will likely get worse before it gets any better.

Getting Back to a Focus on Learning

Bradarich said despite all of the politics—and money to be made with the push for privatization—education has to move back towards a learner-driven model anchored in community. In the past, teachers lived in the neighborhoods where they worked. The students, "they knew you, they talked. Most teachers felt connected to the kids." Today, however, the focus of most schools is on passing the next test—"and the kids can feel it," she said.

"Back in the day, you could capitalize on the strengths" of individual students, she said. The hyper prevalence of standardized "testing changes the whole tone and tenor of the school," and "drives us to the average, and we miss the genius" of individuals, said Bradarich.

Everyone who goes into teaching wants to be accountable for student learning, Bradarich said. Teachers and school leaders believe they should be accountable to students and families and local principalities—not test companies that profit from the $1.7 billion states were estimated to have spent on testing in 2012 (Chingos, 2012). Not only are tests not a true measure of student learning, they ignore students who may have strengths outside of the tested areas, and they often create a deficit model instead of a strength model, Bradarich said. And students of color are most disproportionately impacted.

"You can teach kids how to take the gatekeeping tests later, and teach them to be humans sooner," said Bradarich.

"You Can Do It"

In HISD, some schools don't have the funds to take students on field trips at all, and in many places, all of the arts and computer programs have been cut because of staffing and budget issues, thanks to the reliance on local taxes. But Bradarich believes districts should be leveraging the strengths of individual schools to promote equity across the district— schools with more resources should partner with those with fewer resources to share services and offerings between them. Having teachers and principals who have cross-linear experiences and can share and learn from each other how to best serve the populations within their schools can help raise achievement for all students.

But the challenge, she said, is figuring out "how do we share that authentically, because the sum is greater than the parts."

"Every kid needs one person in the building who sees them," said Bradarich. "Everybody needs someone to connect with."

Parent engagement can be hard, because "there's more vulnerability, more generational hopelessness, and when you call, it's 'I don't want to hear, that, because I'm doing the best I can,'" said Bradarich. But adults in the building can model how to have respectful conversations, which are driven by relationships and a mutual respect for each others' opinions and experiences. And if conversations with both students and family members are framed in the context of respect and caring and having confidence the students can achieve with a little help, rather than making families feel defensive about the shortcomings of their children, families are more likely to support school efforts, she said.

For its part, Houston Community College is working to figure out how to get students to see themselves as college material and making sure they have the right supports in place when those students arrive. "We're an open-access institution, so getting accepted isn't really the deal—it's giving them a piece of paper to say 'you're accepted, you can do it, and here's someone who can help you,'" said Houston Community College Vice Chancellor for Planning and Institutional Effectiveness Kurt Ewen.

For HCC President Caesar Maldonado, the emphasis on student support and success is even more important to his hiring decisions than trying to attract the preeminent subject matter experts. "I want the best person who's going to accomplish the mission [and] take the content and put it in the context of the mission that will help our students succeed," he said.

Seven in 10 Houston Community College students are in need of remediation when they arrive, which Ewen said is reflective of the pipeline coming out of the Houston Independent School District. "These kids are in an ecosystem," he said. "The metric is not graduation rates, the metric is student success, and that looks different depending on where students are."

Still, graduation rates have to be a big part of the conversation. "In no other industry would you look at a 20% yield on your work" and be satisfied, said Maldonado, who was a systems engineer before heading into higher ed.

The short-term goal is to get trade certificates issued to students in HISD who may have dropped out of high school at some point. Working with a number of local and regional leaders, HCC is partnering with HISD to increase the number of career pipelines for students while reducing the number of contact hours required to get students on the job—in some cases, programs that can be completed in one summer, he said. One challenge to this, however, is what Ewen calls "perverse funding models" that actually incentivize longer completion times by allocating dollars based on contact hours.

The system is also helping to establish academies to boost K–12 students' college readiness, and is committed to working with the district long-term to help reform the pipeline overall.

"If there's something that's going to happen in Houston, we're going to be a part of it," Maldonado said. "Whether officially, or just showing up and knocking on the door saying we're here to help."

REFERENCES

Binkovitz, L. (2018, May 23). *Of the 21 largest school districts in Texas, none matched the national average for per student spending.* Retrieved https://kinder.rice.edu/2018/05/22/when-it-comes-student-spending-and-state-funding-houston-and-other-large-texas-school

Chingos, M. (2012, November 29). *Strength in numbers: State spending on K–12 Assessment Systems.* Retrieved https://www.brookings.edu/research/strength-in-numbers-state-spending-on-k-12-assessment-systems/

DeVries, N. (2017, November 28). Texas Academic Performance Reports. Retrieved from https://tea.texas.gov/perfreport/tapr/index.html

Gorski, P. (2015, October 14). Imagining equity literacy. Retrieved from https://www.tolerance.org/magazine/imagining-equity-literacy?elq=b0d17e3485b44c4c92b12ba1da290178&elq CampaignId=248

Houston ISD. 2017–2018 Facts and figures. (n.d.). Retrieved from http://www.houstonisd.org/ achievements

Klineberg, S. L. (2018). *Kinder Houston Area Survey 2018.* Houston, TX: Kinder Institute for Urban Research. Retrieved from https://kinder.rice.edu/sites/g/files/bxs1676/f/documents/Kinder%20Houston%20Area%20Survey%202018.pdf

Largest school districts in America. (n.d.). Retrieved from https://www.niche.com/k12/search/ largest-school-districts/

Marder, M., & Villanueva, C. (2017, October). *Consequences of the Texas Public School Funding Hole of 2011–16.* Retrieved https://forabettertexas.org/images/EO_2017_09_SchoolFinance_ALL.pdf

Mejia, B. (2017, May 9). How Houston has become the most diverse place in America. *Los Angeles Times.* Retrieved from http://www.latimes.com/nation/la-na-houston-diversity-2017-htmlstory.html

School Reform Initiative. (2016). Equity statement. Retrieved from http://www.schoolreform initiative.org/equity-statement-2/

U.S. Census. (2017). QuickFacts: Houston city, Texas. Retrieved from https://www.census.gov/ quickfacts/fact/table/houstoncitytexas/PST045217

CHAPTER 8

MILWAUKEE

INTRODUCTION

There are few things more dichotomous than the educational experience in the city of Milwaukee.

I attended Samuel Morse Middle School for the Gifted and Talented during Grades 6–8. The natural progression from there was to attend Rufus King High School, considered the best high school in Milwaukee at the time. That's the path most of my friends and classmates took. I chose to attend North Division High School, a school known now, and even back then as the worst in the city. My reason for choosing North Division was because of the fabulous arts program that provided me with my first chance to experience New York City and opportunities to perform around the city and other parts of the country. My high school years are still some of the best years of my life. The school was and is still over 97% African American. It was my first opportunity to be surrounded by African American people all day, every day. My self-confidence and pride in myself and my culture skyrocketed. I was active and busy in shows, activities, traveling, camping. I took every opportunity that came my way. And I had such a great experience that I spent 9 years of my education career working to replicate that experience for other high school students.

What was lost on me at the time is that there were students in the same high school as mine having a very different experience. They weren't being

---

given the same opportunities. They weren't singing and performing and traveling throughout their time at North Division. In fact, most students weren't. When I entered as a ninth grade student, there were about 1,500 students in the school. I graduated just a few short years later from a class of 89 students.

That was the state of education in Milwaukee in 1992, I am sad to say, that is still the state of education in Milwaukee today.

Almost 30 years later, Rufus King is one of the highest performing high schools in the city and North Division is still the lowest performing the city. Only now, when I walk the halls of North Division as an alum and education professional, I can feel the disparity in the darkness of the windowless building, the scarcity of students in a big building with such great potential.

In spite of the many efforts in the city of Milwaukee to transform education, our reality is still this:

- NAEP fourth grade reading exam scores in Wisconsin scores have been statistically flat since 1992.
- All racial, socioeconomic, and disability status subgroups perform below the national average for their respective subgroups.
- African American students in the state rank 49th among Black students in the country and White students rank 41st (behind Alabama and Mississippi) among White students.
- Wisconsin has a gap of 32 points between White and Black students, the fifth largest in the country, representing approximately three grade levels.
- 35% of Wisconsin fourth graders score proficient or advanced on the NAEP fourth grade reading test, down from 37% in 2015.
- Milwaukee ranks 25th of 26 national urban districts, with a 30-point White/Black achievement gap.

Milwaukee led the way for other cities in the country to embrace expanded school choice with the Milwaukee Parental Choice Program, allowing families to access vouchers to pay tuition costs for their children to attend private schools. But even after the emergence of charter schools with multiple charter authorizers within our city, open enrollment allowing Milwaukee students to access suburban school districts and Chapter 220—an initiative aimed at integrating our suburban school districts and the Milwaukee Public School district, our reality is a gap between White students and Black students that is the equivalent of three grade levels!

We have national partnerships with organizations like Teach for America, New Leaders for New Schools (which is no longer in Milwaukee) and City Year and have no shortage of nonprofit organizations that have been established with the intent to improve education for our city's children, but we continue to fail. Milwaukee has the second largest achievement gap of all national urban districts, according to NAEP.

The biggest reason I think we continually fail our students is because of the divisive mindsets of those leading the charges within education and education reform and the unwillingness to come together and work from a single plan towards better outcomes for children. Our city needs a plan that embraces options for families and children while also upholding an unwavering quality bar. Instead, many are choosing to fight for territory rather than for children. Choice versus Charter versus District or the teacher's union versus anybody who dares challenge the status quo. Many are choosing ego and to make names for themselves rather than to make better futures for our children, resulting in nonprofits doing duplicative work, competing for resources from the philanthropic community or even from the schools they exist to serve. I believe the chaotic educational landscape we've built and continue to sustain has resulted in inaction, a lack of results and a lack of strategic direction, which is creating confusion for families and exhaustion to the political climate and the philanthropic community. A single, comprehensive plan for our city and the long-term mobilization of parents to advocate for a high quality education for their children could be the game changer this city needs to move forward. If not, it is difficult to anticipate the next 30 years not looking like the last 30 years.

In spite of this, I remain hopeful because I know that there are still people in this city who wake up every day knowing that if we don't stand on behalf of our children, we sentence them to a life of poverty and everything that comes with it. I remain hopeful because I know that if we can ever come together with children at the center, anything is possible. I remain hopeful because while I would like to see improvements for all of our babies, I know that there are pockets of success and lives that are forever changed because of them.

Rashida Evans is a Milwaukee native who has committed herself to improving educational outcomes and opportunities for the Black and brown children in the city who need them the most. A former K–12 administrator, Evans has worked as a school turnaround principal, district administrator, academic director, and dean of students. She is most proud of the seven years she spent as an elementary school teacher. Currently, she serves as Interim Executive Director for Partners Advancing Value in Education and Schools That Can-Milwaukee.

MILWAUKEE

"We Don't Have Failed Schools.
We Have Failed Communities"

A year ago, Milwaukee Public Schools administrators recently realized they have failed students of color on every metric, from test scores to Grade Point Averages to attendance rates to graduation rates. In response, the district created a Department of Black and Latino Male Achievement in the fall of 2017 to try to address some of the gaps.

But Howard Fuller—a Distinguished Professor of Education, founder of Milwaukee Collegiate Academy and a renowned education and civil rights activist in Milwaukee—said the city "has been failing Black children for at least 40 years, if not more."

A group of Milwaukee legislators recently called Wisconsin the worst place in the country to raise a Black child, citing disproportionate incarceration rates and educational inequities as driving their declaration ("Black, Hispanic Lawmakers," 2018). The city is one of the most segregated and unemployment and incarceration rates for Black men are among the highest in the nation. But even more than the segregation patterns, Fuller believes the historic unemployment of Black people in the city is the number one issue facing Milwaukee's Black population.

Jamaal Smith, former Milwaukee NAACP education chair and currently the community engagement manager for YWCA-Southeast Wisconsin, said deindustrialization hit the Rust Belt city hard, and the Black population in particular has not recovered from the loss of factory jobs.

"When it came to working in factories, you could get a high school diploma, go work in a factory, make a very decent wage, buy homes and make a good living" which created a strong middle class and enabled families to invest in the education of their children, he said.

"The alternative following the de-industrialization was low-wage jobs, drugs, guns—so you started to see the erosion of the Black community based on the practices that were beyond the control of the Black community. You started to see a large outward migration of people who believed they could find better opportunities outside of the city," he said, adding that the lack of job opportunities and competitive wages "decimated the Milwaukee workforce for African Americans. This was inevitable, what we see, as far as the high levels of violence, as far as the crime."

The crack cocaine epidemic that ravaged inner cities across the country in the 1980s did not spare Milwaukee, and it brought with it companion issues like high rates of teenage pregnancy and higher incarceration rates that also plagued other cities in the '80s and early '90s. In 2010, Wisconsin had the highest percentage of incarcerated Black men of any of the states—in Milwaukee County, more than half of Black men in their 30s have spent time in prison ("Project Milwaukee," 2016).

"When you put people in desperate situations who were at one point able to sustain themselves and make a decent living on their own, then you're going to find other ways to survive," Smith said.

Michelle Carter, a public school principal in Milwaukee, said many of today's students were born to parents who were a product of that turmoil in the '80s and '90s, and the struggles of many of the parents have impacted the "emphasis on making sure kids are supported and have everything they need to get a quality education."

"Milwaukee likes to talk a lot about the educational problem and put a lot of blame on schools, but they really don't want to tackle the outside circumstances—you only deal with and control the things that are in your environment. You can't control the things that are in the home, and … it's becoming very difficult to combat mental health issues [and] overcome academic deficits from years of being passed along" in the case of many of the students, she said. "And there's not money to provide layers of support so that they can even make it back to the level that they're supposed to be on."

"We Don't Have Failed Schools. We Have Failed Communities"

Smith said racist policies in the city have "decimated Black families, Black entrepreneurship, Black advancement economically, and that has trickled down to impact the children—and particularly their advancement in school," he said. "We don't have failed schools; we have failed communities."

Many of the Black families who make over $100,000 per year still live in lower-income neighborhoods—a phenomenon a group of Stanford researchers refer to as the neighborhood gap (Reardon, Fox, & Townsend, 2015). (see Figure 8.1.)

Smith said in some cases, this is because families still believe in the neighborhoods they grew up in and want to stay and improve them, but in others, "You have [families] who don't want to expose themselves or their children to the bias or the racism that would be prevalent if they were to move into white neighborhoods."

Smith said fear of how their children will be treated, how they'll be received, what the response would be if the family had a gathering and the music was louder than the neighbors thought acceptable keeps families from changing neighborhoods. "Many of them, instead of exposing themselves or their children to that type of backlash, they just stay within the city limits," Smith said. However, the spacial inequality, in terms of the concentration of resources and opportunities needed for people to survive being concentrated outside of the city, has meant that "not only are people lacking in jobs with adequate wages, but the opportunities are not there for people to purchase the products and services that are needed."

"When you couple that with sending students to school and asking them to perform, you are asking our young people a lot. We have to start looking at the entire aspect of what our young people deal with and become more empathetic and realizing what they're dealing with and figure out ways that we can benefit the student as a whole," said Smith.

Carter said when she was growing up in Milwaukee in the '70s, schools were often understaffed—"It was very much the norm to have substitute teachers in urban classrooms," sometimes for an entire school year, she said. "How are kids expected to be successful if they are not being serviced by credentialed teachers, or there is a lot of change back and forth," she asked.

When integration came in the 1970s, the thought was some of the problems facing the city's schools would be resolved, but that did not happen, said Fuller. "If you look at NAEP scores, you look at whatever it is you want to use as indicators, it is clear that poor Black children are being failed."

According to Lanelle Ramey, director of Milwaukee Public Schools' Department of Black and Latino Male Achievement, part of the issue is the lack of strong, Black business community and strong Black narrative for youth in the city to look up to and help control the narrative in the city. And "because we deal with hyper segregation too, the trust is very limited," when it comes to citizens' trust of any institution, including schools, he said.

"The main problem is I don't think that Black children are valued in this country," said Fuller, who pointed out that "The system was never set up to educate us in the first place. So in essence, to educate our kids is like a revolutionary act."

Fuller said educators have to be prepared to contend with challenges around "all of the things that happen to kids before they ever get to school and the enduring problem of once they get in here, do we have the correct teaching and learning strategy" to serve them.

For example, Fuller said his salutatorian this past year has had to contend with a mother who has been in prison for murder since the girl was very young. She managed to get accepted into 26 colleges, but she also recently found out she's pregnant.

And the valedictorian and her mother have faced homelessness off and on at various points throughout her schooling.

"All of these [outside] things impact their ability to learn, but at the same time, people are fiercely protecting the existing structures, not because they are working for our kids academically, but because these systems are job engines," Fuller said.

"The question is how do you educate our children for the 21st century— what is it that we need to be doing. It's a given that a significant number of our children are poor," he said. "We really have to be real about what is actually happening to us as a people, when it comes to education, and then how our struggle for education is impacted by every other aspect of our oppression as a people."

Carter said, "It's an adult problem that we can't wrap our arms around from a city perspective." She said outgoing superintendent Darienne Driver "did an amazing job of getting the story out about who our students are" and had just started to move beyond the surface level in her efforts to attract the support of business leaders around the city. Business leaders were just starting to establish real relationships, beyond one-time donations or occasional volunteers, according to Carter, who worries the momentum may have been disturbed by the school board's decision to change leadership directions again.

"The commitment from businesses in the city—it really is an all-hands-on-deck kind of thing. There are ways that we can get families involved in schools, and it's like people are afraid to really push that and get it done. We've got to find more meaningful ways to really push that and get people involved, Carter said.

Building a Culture of Respect

Milwaukee Collegiate is a Black-led school. The principal is Black, the board is majority-Black. And Fuller said he thinks the reason the school has been so successful—100% of the school's students have been accepted into college 6 year in a row—is because school leaders and teachers have "worked hard to build a culture of mutual respect for kids and for educators in the building. "There's a relentless focus on our children and loving them even when they're not lovable."

Fuller is a big proponent of the personalized learning approach, and "an absolute commitment to our kids." A personalized approach requires students to take a lot of responsibility for their own learning, but it also "requires a different kind of a teacher," he said. Teachers who see themselves as the ticket to students' salvation are not likely to be successful in leading a personalized classroom, but those who see themselves as facilitators and guides of learning, and who respect the students' ability to drive the process for themselves are key, Fuller said.

"Having educators who, and the predominant number of our teachers are white, but they're people who actually have high expectations for our kids, believe they can learn and they're committed" also makes a huge difference. "And the ones who don't, we get rid of them."

Carter said it is not to be assumed that people of color are automatically more culturally responsive—differences in socioeconomic status still have an impact on teachers' ability to relate to students—but she believes there is something to be said for students being able to see people who look like them in leadership roles.

When students step into a classroom and see the same kinds of racist thinking that governs the city as a whole, said Smith, not only does it add to the frustration and anger students feel as a result of their circumstances, it impacts the children physically and psychologically and impedes their ability to learn.

"You have to create a school where, one, when kids come into the school, they have a sense of belonging, that the school is really their place, and two, that there's some sense of autonomy, so the kids are not driven entirely by rules," said Fuller. And third, he said, it's important that there is a focus on competency to make sure students are actually learning.

Ramey said the most important thing in a city like Milwaukee—or any place that serves a high population of students of color—is putting culturally responsive teaching practices at the forefront of everything in the school. From when students walk in the door to every interaction they have during the school day, when they leave to return the next morning, Ramey said cultural responsiveness needs to be incorporated into every part of the educational experience.

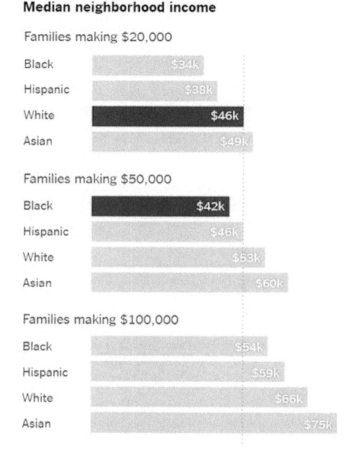

Median neighborhood income

Families making $20,000

Black — $34k
Hispanic — $38k
White — $46k
Asian — $49k

Families making $50,000

Black — $42k
Hispanic — $46k
White — $53k
Asian — $60k

Families making $100,000

Black — $54k
Hispanic — $59k
White — $66k
Asian — $75k

Source: Reardon, Fox, and Townsend (2015).

Figure 8.1.   Milwaukee has what researchers call a "neighborhood gap."

There's no approach that works for all students, and even with the approaches that work for most students, Fuller believes the most important aspect of education reform is changing the non-school factors that impact students in the city. "If you ask me what is the most important thing, it's raise the minimum wage to $15," he said. "If you change the economic circumstances of our children, that actually has a broader impact than some of the things that we do in schools." School leaders can make great strides during the day, but "it would be better for my kids not to be poor, it would be better for my kids to have clothes and food and stuff like that," said Fuller.

REFERENCES

Black, Hispanic lawmakers call Wisconsin worst place in nation to raise a Black child. (2018, February 12). *Fox 6 Now*. Retrieved from https://fox6now. com/2018/02/12/Black-hispanic-lawmakers-call-wisconsin-worst-place-in-nation-to-raise-a-Black-child/

Reardon, S. F., Fox, L., & Townsend, J. (2015). Neighborhood income composition by household race and income, 1990–2009. *The ANNALS of the American Academy of Political and Social Science,660*(1), 78–97. doi:10.1177/0002716215576104

Project Milwaukee: Black Men in Prison [Radio series episode]. (2016). Milwaukee, WI: WUWM & MPTV.

CHAPTER 9

NEW ORLEANS

INTRODUCTION

Every child. Every school. Every day. We endeavor to provide every child with the best school environment every day. This is our charge as a school district and it is a charge that I happily lead as Superintendent of Orleans Parish public schools.

The Orleans Parish School Board (OPSB) oversees 75 charter schools, two direct operated schools and a school with two educational programs for students in secure care facilities. Within our 78 schools, we serve about 45,000 students; 83% of our students are Black, and 83% of our students are economically disadvantaged.

When we fall short of our focus on providing a quality education for every child in every school every day, our community suffers the consequences. Unfortunately, in New Orleans, one in 14 Black men are in prison, and 90% of the people incarcerated in our city are Black. These statistics are a deafening reminder that the school district must continue to find ways to abolish the school-to-prison pipeline and work to create systematic change that empowers students and their families.

The history of public schools in Orleans Parish has been well documented and spotlighted after Hurricane Katrina. Before and after the storm, the equity and achievement gaps for low-income students of color have been pervasive. In 2004, only 24% of New Orleans students were

Let's Stop Calling It an Achievement Gap, pp. 93–104
Copyright © 2019 by Information Age Publishing
All rights of reproduction in any form reserved.

achieving basic proficiency on state tests. Following the storm, the state took control of schools and began the process of chartering schools over the years. The actions taken by the state in the past decade have led us to a nearly fully chartered public-school system in the city of New Orleans. Public schools in Orleans Parish were set on a course to try to increase performance of students under the two systems, with two different governing bodies and multiple sets of rules by which operators had to implement programming and other services for students. For more than 10 years, public schools struggled to raise test scores, address student, family, and teacher needs, while also responding to the myriad of state standardized achievement levels by which "success" would be measured.

When I joined the OPSB in March of 2015, we were operating under a fragmented system. There were two separate entities running the district— the Recovery School District (RSD), which operated under the auspices of the Louisiana State Board of Education, and the locally elected Orleans Parish School Board. We were a system of traditional schools, direct-run schools and charter schools with both the RSD and the OPSB overseeing several of each. Over the years, through these fragmented systems, we have made progress specifically for Black students, but we still have a long way to go. Nevertheless, as of July 1, all schools in the district were once again unified under the jurisdiction and oversight of the locally elected Orleans Parish School Board.

In the past 12 years the high school graduation rate has increased 20%, the student eligibility rate for the college state scholarship (TOPS) has increased and more New Orleans public school students are attending college than before. New Orleans is now the national leader in Black male graduation rates.

A guiding principle of the newly unified school district and a continued strategic priority of the OPSB is that every family should have access to a diverse set of school options for their children. Currently, there are not enough good options for our families. This is unacceptable, and we have worked to reorganize the role of the school board to address this issue. This means that each year we will seek to ensure that any decision to open, close, expand, or consolidate a school throughout the city has an effect of increasing the diversity of program types so that each student can find a school that is right for them. Increasing that diversity also means that our school system includes schools that honor the culture and traditions of our city and uphold the legacy of generations that have come before.

Efforts extend beyond the classroom as well. We are excited to know that at our Youth Study Center school—the school operated in our youth detention center—we are getting much better results with a high-quality, nationally recognized operator. That also means partnering with nonprofit organizations to launch a centralized, multi-million-dollar, career and technical education center.

Under our new unified system, we will also be able to provide support to schools in a way we haven't been able to before. With the creation of the School Support and Improvement Office, we will help struggling schools find needed resources to push high quality instruction. With our unique position, we are able to find ways to address broader unmet needs citywide.

Even with these successes, we know that 50% of Black children in New Orleans still live in poverty and that all public schools in our district are still not performing where we want them to be. There are no easy solutions, but this school board and this administration will continue to fight to ensure that all students receive a quality and lasting education. If we give the next generation a chance to learn and grow, they will show us the way into the future.

Every child. Every school. Every day. This is our promise.

Dr. Henderson Lewis, Jr. is Superintendent of Schools for the Orleans Parish School Board.

NEW ORLEANS

A Total Eclipse of Local Control— and How Reform Efforts Have Failed Our Students

When Hurricane Katrina hit the gulf coast of the United States, hundreds of thousands of people in Mississippi, Alabama and Louisiana were displaced, and institutions and families across the city are still trying to recover from the damage. No place was hit harder than New Orleans, where already vulnerable levees collapsed and the waters from Lake Pontchartrain, Lake Borgne and several lakes and marshes rushed into the city. New Orleans was all but wiped out—and so was its public-school system, which would reemerge in the months after the storm as a state-operated, totally-charter system which eliminated local control and set a blueprint for one of the most aggressive urban school reform plans in the country (Brown, 2015).

In the 2004–2005 school year—the year immediately before Katrina hit—71% of the city's teachers were Black. In the 2013–2014 school year, that number had dropped to 49%. More than half of this change took place right after the storm, when all of the city's 7,000 teachers were fired to make room for the new system. Few were rehired, which set the pattern for "a steady reduction" in the proportion of Black teachers hired, while the city saw an increase of White teachers hired (Barrett & Harris, 2015).

"In New Orleans, a city that's rooted in culture and tradition ... these people came from out of town, and they can't relate and they're criminalizing our students who don't adhere to their exact standards of discipline," said Tania Roubion, who taught in New Orleans pre- and post-Katrina.

Before Katrina, the Orleans Parish school district ranked 67th of 68th out of Louisiana school districts. The percentage of students in poverty in the district, 38%, was 15% higher than the state overall (Subberwal, 2017). By all accounts, the district had the same issues most inner city district had after desegregation: White flight saw the majority of the middle- to upper class white families taking their children out of the schools in New Orleans and upper class and poor and working class whites alike moved to the suburbs around the city to keep their children from being schooled with Black children.

But long-time educators in the city say there were positives. The district, led by a predominantly Black board, adopted a "60–40 rule," which said 60% of teachers and staff in a majority-Black school had to be Black, and vice versa. Teachers came from the communities where their students lived and had a vested personal interest in the success of the students. Despite having fewer resources and lower test scores, Roubion believes students were learning more than they are today.

"When you look at people [in their late 30s and early 40s], they're intelligent, they can form complete sentences, evaluate, critically think. And we're creating a generation of robotic children who" are getting into college at higher rates, but who seem comparatively less intelligent, she said.

But not everyone agrees. In fact, some believe there was never a point when schools in New Orleans were adequate, at least as it pertains to the education of the city's Black students. Robert Collins, a professor of urban studies and public policy at Dillard University in New Orleans was raised by a mother who taught in Orleans Parish schools for over 40 years, but who would not send her own children to the city's public schools, opting, as even most middle-class Black families did, to send Collins and his siblings to private school instead.

After "A Nation at Risk" was released in 1983, schools were increasingly judged by test scores and, like in many other places, many all-Black schools were labeled failing schools and closed, and students were bussed to the other side of town for school. Even private schools, newly subject to the state assessments because of their initial decision to accept vouchers, had lower test scores than were deemed acceptable, and they eventually opted out of the voucher system, favoring their reputations over any small influx of state money.

After the Storm

Then came Katrina, which evacuated nearly 80% of the city's residents. In the aftermath, Black residents remained mostly displaced; Black residents were significantly less likely to have returned to New Orleans within a year of the storm than non-Blacks were, at 44%, versus 67% of non-Blacks (Sastry & Gregory, 2012), mostly because of a lack of affordable housing. (Houston took in the largest population of those displaced by Katrina, herding a majority of the evacuees "in FEMA-funded apartments in high-crime, high-poverty neighborhoods on the city's southwest side" (Bliss, 2015).

Students missed anywhere from months to a whole year of school, and many found themselves in several schools in the same year. Families moved an average of 3.5 times in the 8 months that immediately followed the storm (Redlener & Schang, 2006). According to a 2007 report from the Southern Education Foundation, one in five school-age children were either not enrolled in school or were only partially attending, missing 10 or more days per month in the 2005–2006 school year, and between 20,000 and 30,000 students did not attend school at all that year (Education After Katrina, n.d.). As many as 10,000–15,000 missed most or all days of school in the 2006–2007 school year as well. The report also found the schools that absorbed these students in all 49 other states had insufficient funds, supplies, personnel and classroom space to adequately care for these students, and reported an increase in disciplinary problems as well as a need for more mental health services. Between 45,000 and 54,000 students dropped out of college for at least one semester; many transferred to schools in other major cities like Houston and Atlanta, but low-income and Black college students had the most difficult time transferring. Two dozen public and private colleges in New Orleans and along the Gulf Coast of Mississippi closed (Education After Katrina, n.d.).

According to Collins, "80% of the real estate in the city of New Orleans was not inhabitable after Katrina. Even if in theory there were schools that were able to open, it would not have been really practical to even have a school open."

"It was a very disruptive year to those students," he said. "And not just a disruptive year, but even though the students could return to their schools the following year, their parents couldn't come back, because maybe their businesses couldn't re-open" or they couldn't find affordable housing, so in many cases, "it took them two, three, four, five years to get back, because, again, the whole family unit has to come back."

A student who was just starting second grade when Katrina hit would have been more likely than his peers in all but two cities to be unemployed and out of school at 17, according to a Tulane University study that examined the state of the "Katrina Generation" (Fothergill & Peek, 2015).

Roubion said, "I feel kind of responsible—all of the kids who were sold a dream and now they're sitting on their front porch not doing anything."

Shan Williams, who has worked as a teacher and school administrator since 1971, said when "we as a people left" because of the storm, "you had another group of people that stayed and planned and had all these educational ideas." The district had been taken over by the state, and under a white governor and legislature, had approved the recovery school district, which was never intended to be run by the residents of the city.

"The powers that be who don't look like me in the mirror are telling me that they know how to raise my kids better than I do," said Williams, expressing a frustration that can be heard among educators across the city.

Williams acknowledges the previous system was failing, but says the current system isn't any better; the only difference now is whites in the city and in the state have all the power. "We don't control anything anymore," he said, unconvinced that the city's students are any better off than they were under the previous leadership team, which was anchored by a Black mayor and Black school board. "They're not just shooting Blacks in Pittsburgh and such, they're doing this in the schools. They're not shooting with bullets, they're shooting with education," Williams said.

More Than Just a Charter Versus Neighborhood Schools Debate

Williams said the biggest issue with New Orleans' charter system is that most of the schools aren't raising additional money to support efforts in the schools, and a recent study from the Education Research Alliance for New Orleans found that New Orleans schools spend 13% more on administrative and operating expenses than other schools, meaning the money the schools do have is not going towards teaching and learning (Jewson, 2017). What the researchers found is that when you decentralize an entire district, schools lose the economies of scale that would come from procuring needed services and operating costs as part of a conglomerate.

"True charters have a board that helps raise money to support the school, plus get money from the state or federal government—that doesn't happen in the Black charter schools," Williams said.

The same study found that while administrators often make much more than their traditional school counterparts, teachers are paid less and receive fewer benefits, which Collins attributes to the lack of a union for these teachers. Teachers have largely lost the benefit of a pension—those who had enough years invested before the change are still eligible, but any new teacher hired into the system only has the option of a private retirement account, Collins said.

But the biggest gripe in New Orleans and a number of other cities that have heavy charter school presences is the lack of consistency in the credentialing requirements for teachers.

"One teacher is a convicted felon for drug distribution and he's teaching now. They glamorize it, because they say he's able to tell the kids what not to do. Pre-Katrina if you had any kind of record, especially a convicted felon, we couldn't hire you. Now, it's like anything goes," said Williams. "Us older people say if we had the leeway and the unlimited power that the schools have now, we never would have gotten into a situation where we had failing schools."

No Confidence in the City's Schools

In conversation after conversation with educators and researchers alike, no one could cite a school in New Orleans—other than magnet schools which had selective admissions or private schools—where they'd feel comfortable sending their children. Despite a rise in test scores, the overall sentiment about the effectiveness in public education in the city is the same or lower than it was pre-Katrina. Teachers report working more hours and lower levels of satisfaction—and Black teachers report larger average declines in job satisfaction than any others—and teachers who taught in the city before Katrina hit comprise only 10% of the total workforce today (Weixler, Harris, & Barrett, 2017).

Collins said it is true that there are fewer low-performing schools in the city than there were two decades ago, "but the reason [the district has] fewer low-performing schools is because they have fewer schools, period. They merged [and closed] a lot of the neighborhood schools. Now you don't have three low-performing schools, you just have one low-performing school, but it's because you closed down two of those schools," he said.

And the distribution of those schools remains unchanged. "I can point to a map and tell you where the low-performing schools are going to be, and 90% of the time I'm right—it's whether or not it's going to be located in a distressed neighborhood. And I've seen no evidence that those schools in those distressed neighborhoods are doing any better under the charter system than they were doing under the old Orleans Parish School" board, he said.

"Those kids have unique sets of problems, and if you don't deal with those unique problems that the students are having—you need to feed them, you need extra counseling, extra social workers, because their parents might be dealing with substance abuse, [students] might be dealing with substance abuse themselves. You have to provide special resources to these kids in these schools," said Collins, who believes both systems have failed the city's poor, Black residents equally.

Williams said the open enrollment system, which has students traveling across wards to go to school, has caused an increase in violence as well. Murders were down 10 years after Katrina, but crimes like robbery and rape had increased, and the population was significantly diminished (Mackel, 2015).

Making Connections

"When I started teaching [in 1971], I thought I could save them all," said Williams, who now works as an assistant principal at Landry-Walker High School. I'm not tired yet, but the adults in this whole education situation are kind of making me tired. … But my love for teaching and my love for working with kids supersedes that. I come in here and do what I need to do for those children."

Williams said he leverages Landry-Walker's reputation as having a top football program to lure students in and all but tricks them into excelling academically as well. "We suck them in [on the promise of athletics] and we rein them in academically," he said.

"Parent involvement can only go so far," said Williams. "It's limited, because the parents are not educated enough to help, so you've got to help the parents."

As the state looks to transition power back to the Orleans Parish School Board, advocates and educators are skeptical. "Somehow they're saying the power is going to be equalized," said Williams. The long-term plan is for the charter schools to now answer directly to the Orleans Parish School Board, but Collins says the change will be gradual, because "we're in a political transition phase right now."

"Over the years, we've had some incompetent folks run the school system, but the good thing about it was, when people did a bad job, you could vote people out," he said. Now, there's no local accountability, and the consensus is, there's also a decline in school pride from a community standpoint.

"Here's the reality: That K–12 education, that's what makes or breaks these kids' chances in life. By the time they get to the university, their lot in life is pretty much already established," said Collins. "I was a visiting professor at Harvard, and it's not that they're doing a great job of teaching, it's that they're taking kids who were already basically the valedictorian of their class and they're polishing them up a little bit, giving them a little bit of social skills and the network, but you didn't make them brilliant."

But for other institutions, especially historically Black colleges and universities said Collins, "we get a lot of kids who are just not prepared. And then we spend the first few years just trying to break them of their bad habits that they learned in their K–12 system."

"By the time we get them, for the most part, their range of accomplishments has already been determined," Collins said. "We try to work with them and bring them up as much as we can, but it's difficult if the K–12 system has not prepared them well."

And the reality, he said, is many of "those kids are not going to graduate in four years."

REFERENCES

Barrett, N., & Harris, D. (2015, August 24). *Significant changes in the New Orleans teacher workforce* Retrieved https://educationresearchalliancenola.org/files/publications/ERA-Policy-Brief-Changes-in-the-New-Orleans-Teacher-Workforce.pdf

Bliss, L. (2015, August 25). 10 years later, there's so much we don't know about where Katrina survivors ended up. *CityLab*. Retrieved from https://www.citylab.com/equity/2015/08/10-years-later-theres-still-a-lot-we-dont-know-about-where-katrina-survivors-ended-up/401216/

Brown, E. (2015, September 3). Katrina swept away New Orleans school system, ushering in new era. *The Washington Post*. Retrieved from https://www.washingtonpost.com/news/education/wp/2015/09/03/katrina-swept-away-new-orleans-school-system-ushering-in-new-era/?utm_term=.deef2117d381

Education after Katrina. (n.d.). Retrieved from http://www.southerneducation.org/Our-Research/Research-and-Publications/Education-after-Katrina-(1)/Education-after-Katrina-Executive-Summary.aspx

Fothergill, A., & Peek, L. A. (2015). *Children of Katrina*. Austin, TX: University of Texas Press.

Jewson, M. (2017, January 17). Study says New Orleans schools spend more on administration and less on teaching after charter transformation. Retrieved from https://thelensnola.org/2017/01/17/study-says-new-orleans-schools-spend-more-on-administration-and-less-on-teaching-after-charter-transformation/

Mackel, T. (2015, August 10). 10 years forward: Is New Orleans safer after Katrina? New Orleans, LA: WDSU 6 News. Retrieved from https://www.wdsu.com/article/10-years-forward-is-new-orleans-safer-after-katrina/3379077

Redlener, I. E., & Schang, G. (2006). *Responding to an emerging humanitarian crisis in Louisiana and Mississippi: Urgent need for health care "Marshall Plan."* New York, NY: The Children's Health Fund. doi:https://doi.org/10.7916/D8VD76V8

Sastry, N., & Gregory, J. (2012). The location of displaced New Orleans residents in the year after Hurricane Katrina. *SSRN Electronic Journal*. doi:10.2139/ssrn.2201806

Subberwal, K. (2017, August 30). Harvey's impact on students could be felt 'For Generations'. *Huffington Post*. Retrieved from https://www.huffingtonpost.com/entry/hurricane-katrina-harvey-schools_us_59a725d7e4b0a8d14572e0ec

Weixler, L.B., Harris, D. N., & Barrett, N. (2017, May 9). *Teachers' perspectives on learning and work environments under the New Orleans School Reforms.* Retrieved https://educationresearchalliancenola.org/publications/teachers-perspectives-on-learning-and-work-environments-under-the-new-orleans-school-reforms

CHAPTER 10

PHILADELPHIA

INTRODUCTION

Pennsylvania is considered the "Keystone State"—a designation that implies it was a central part of the America we now know; a foundational piece, a piece that locks in all other components. Unfortunately, for many children in Philadelphia, academic outcomes do not represent the keystone of Pennsylvania's policies. Actually, if you're White or affluent, your educational prospects are pretty good. For those who are forced to attend many of our neighborhood schools—many of them predominantly Black—the odds are systemically stacked against them.

The disparities facing our children can most often start in two main tributaries: racist funding formulas and a pervasive and paralyzing belief gap. These twin towers of oppression feed off of each other. Racial biases tell legislators that Black children aren't worth investing in because they can't achieve anyway. When students lack the outcomes their more affluent peers have, these same legislators point to the data and smugly tell themselves their initial premise, despite it being saturated in falsities, was correct—no need to provide adequate resources. Once again families have sued the state asking for fairness in funding our children's education. Despite the fact that the state constitution dictates that the Pennsylvania legislature "shall provide for the maintenance and support of a thorough and efficient system of public education to serve the needs of the commonwealth," our students have never seen this in action.

Let's Stop Calling It an Achievement Gap, pp. 105–115
Copyright © 2019 by Information Age Publishing
All rights of reproduction in any form reserved.

While we wait for the Pennsylvania Supreme Court to tilt the scales of justice (not a given, as the Pennsylvania Supreme Court refused to hear a similar case years ago) in favor of children, plenty of Pennsylvania legislators believe that a quality education is not guaranteed by the constitution. The lawyers defending the state against this lawsuit believe that it is beyond the state's purview to provide a quality education. And, despite the overwhelming evidence that Black children are getting the short end of the stick, they throw their legislative hands in the air and shrug their shoulders, Oh, well. Tough.

The constitutions of many states only obligate districts to open schools, but do not go so far as to suggest individual students have any constitutional right to a specific level of educational quality. Some believe that funding is no longer an issue because, as legislators frequently trumpet, the state does have a weighted funding formula. But what they are reluctant to reveal is that only 6% of all the money spent on education goes through this "fair" funding formula—94% of the funds continue to be distributed unfairly. Again, a smack in the face for Black children and their communities. It should be noted that Pennsylvania ranks 46th in the country in how it funds its public schools. The bottom of the country. Despicable.

The belief gap, an oppressive, pernicious chasm between what Black students are capable of and what people believe about them, is pervasive and akin to quicksand. Our neighborhood schools are indicative of these low expectations—mainly because they aren't changing. According to Pew Charitable Trust, currently, 61% of our city's ninth graders attend public schools that have some type of admission requirement. That leaves a significant number of freshmen who are zip code bound—often in schools that do provide the education or support necessary to pursue their dreams. Many of these schools have 4-year graduations rates that hover below 70%. In fact, the majority of the neighborhood high schools that over 3,000 freshmen attend are rated as poor quality by the School District of Philadelphia. Multiply that by 10 years—a short dash on the timeline in regards to how many years some of these schools have been producing poor outcomes—and we have a system calcifying a Black and uneducated underclass.

A significant impact must be made in our neighborhood schools to ensure that all students, including the 39% who do not get chosen for a special-admit school, have the education and the corresponding opportunities and experiences to help them determine, pursue, and attain their postsecondary goals. Black students face other aspects of inequity as well. Very few of them will see someone who looks like them at the front of the classroom. Across the state, 96% of all teachers are White. Ninety-six percent. In Philadelphia, while there are significantly more Black teachers, the number still pales in comparison to the number of Black students.

This lack of diversity is oppressive because of the overwhelming research that proves that students need to see mirror images of themselves, not just windows to the White world, in their classrooms and schools. More Black teachers—the conscious types—can decrease the belief gaps that exist in schools and set higher expectations for their students. Black students who have more Black teachers are suspended and pushed out of school less, have more access to rigorous courses, and are more likely to graduate high school and consider college. It seems like a no-brainer to pursue diversification of our state's teaching force—but because it has been ignored for so long, currently, this lack of diverse teachers is a deeply entrenched problem. We also know that a diverse teaching staff isn't just good for Black students. It is good for White teachers and students as well.

With the return of our district to local control, there is an opportunity to accelerate our students' achievement levels, or to continue to fortify the status quo. Ensuring higher levels of accountability for all schools will unnerve traditionalists and reformers, but it is past time to do what's right for our schools and students. With over 1/3 of Philadelphia's 1.5 million people living in poverty (or deep poverty), we cannot expect schools to do it all alone. However, no improvement will occur without radically addressing our neighborhood schools or the funding that is supposed to support them. We need to increase the funding our schools receive and the belief about what they can accomplish. But, to begin, we need to increase the expectations that we hold for ourselves and the policymakers who impact our students' and our city's futures.

Sharif El-Mekki currently serves as principal of Mastery Charter School-Shoemaker Campus, which serves students in 7–12 grades. A Philadelphia native and the son of an educator and an activist, El-Mekki believes education and activism go hand-in-hand.

PHILADELPHIA

Social Justice as Racial Justice and Educators' Fight to Take Back Their City

In 2015, Pennsylvania was ranked as having the widest funding gap between rich and poor districts in the country (Graham, 2015). In the 2016–2017 school year, The School District of Philadelphia spent $9,062 per student excluding construction costs, while the typical wealthy school district in Pennsylvania spent $15,748 (Hanna, 2018). According to Census data, it is the poorest big city in the country, and one-third of the children in the city are living in poverty.

When Superintendent William R. Hite took over in 2012, he inherited mountainous financial challenges—there was uncertainty about whether some schools would even be able to open some years. There were schools without nurses and counselors, and the district had cut art and music in many schools.

According to Lee Whack, deputy chief of communications for The School District of Philadelphia, "Our revenue was growing at 2% and our expenditures were growing at 4%."

Whack said, "Those days are gone, but we are still in a precarious situation, we are still in a situation where we need to make more investments, we need to make sure we are doing more to help schools improve."

The district is making slow progress towards autonomy—the new school board appointed by Philadelphia Mayor Jim Kinney started July 1 after

17 years of the district being under the state-controlled School Reform Commission.

According to Whack, the arts and music programs have been restored and schools are improving, which he attributes to having a mayor who is a champion for education and who is committed to investing in education. "There's a groundswell of local support for education here, and we are certainly seeing our schools improve," he said.

Not everyone is convinced.

"The school district uses rhetoric to say that these students are getting a certain type of education, but it's always lack of funding, always lack of supplies, they may have older materials, or fragmented materials," said Angela Crawford, a teacher leader at Martin Luther King High School. "So when we historically look at Black students maybe taking a standardized test, their numbers are always historically very low, just because they're not getting the quality of education they usually need."

"Teachers are in Denial About Their Own Racial Biases"

Crawford said a lot of the issue is teachers come in with a "Messiah syndrome" hoping to "save" students from themselves or their environments, but don't take the time to get to know the students or visit them in their environments. They have no idea how to navigate in the city, she said, in fact, Crawford believes many are scared to visit the communities where students live, or spend time in the communities surrounding the school outside of the school day. "If you're too scared to come into the community, then you really shouldn't be teaching at that school," she said.

"I can't teach a child I'm not willing to learn. If I'm not developing relationships or having strategies that [show I understand] research shows Black students are better kinesthetic, visual learners, my students are going to fail because I'm teaching what's best for me, not what's best for my students," she said. "I don't know how you teach someone to want to care about their students. I don't know how you teach empathy," she said.

Not only that, but Crawford believes most are not aware of their own biases, and many, she said, don't have any real knowledge of history from any perspective other than the textbook history, which can be problematic since most textbooks often frame Whites as the victors. Even in conversations and exhibits which acknowledge the oppression of non-White people, there is often an extended effort to include White allies who are painted as saviors of the movement.

"People just don't, they don't get it. Then we have systems where they're punitive—the whole art of teaching a lot of times is removed in the classroom. People get fearful that if they try to—even for people who want to be revolutionary teachers, they're fearful because 'I have this book and I have to teach it just like this book.' And just because it's in the book doesn't mean it's best for our students," she said.

Staffing Concerns

In 2017, the district finally reached an agreement with the city's teachers after a 4-year stalemate, though questions remain about how the district will pay for the salary increases it has promised (Graham, 2017). But officials are hopeful that having a deal done will bring some stability and get the district closer to its anchor goal of having great teachers and leaders in every school. Other anchor goals include having 100% of the district's students graduating ready for college or career, having 100% of eighth graders reading at grade-level, and securing all of the funding needed to run an effective district and ensure there's a great school close to where children live, whether charter or public, without having students bussed across the district to have to find those schools.

Whack said the district is focusing heavily on early literacy as a foundation for making sure students are prepared in 8th and 12th grades, and both public and private investments help to support the goal. But "money doesn't fix absolutely everything," he acknowledged, saying students still have to have teachers and principals in the schools "loving them and bringing them along the way" as well as "families that are participating and pushing them along at home."

Taking Back Their City

In the 1970s, local, state and federal entities threw extra money to the all-Black schools in the city and invested in leadership and staff to make a push for more Black and Latino teachers in an effort to make up for years of underfunding and neglect under the segregated system. Like in many other cities, teaching was a pathway to the middle class for the city's Black citizenry. However, the investment wouldn't last, and neither would the dedication to making the teaching force more reflective of the student population. Research from the Shanker Institute found a greater gap between the number of Black students and teachers exists in charter schools than district schools, but the Hispanic gap is consistent across sectors (Bond, Quintero, Casy, & Di Carlo, 2015). The number of Black teachers decreased by 8%–9% between 2001 and 2012, while the number of White teachers increased "modestly," according to the report.

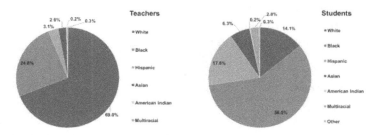

FOOTNOTE TO FIGURE: The "Multiracial" response was available to charter but not district school teachers in 2012, but it is retained in the figure above.

Source: Shanker Institute

Figure 10.1.   Snapshot of Teacher and Student Race and Ethnicity, 2012.

But Black educators in the city are working to take back their city. In the recent elections, two members of the Caucus of Working Educators—a grassroots group of union educators in the city—were voted ward leaders, and others were elected to local neighborhood positions.

Ismael Jimenez, who serves as cochair of the caucus, said, "In Philadelphia, there's been a lot of the status quo politics, a lot of people who play lip service to equity in education but no real substantial thing has been done, just kind of tweaking around the edges." Now, "there is a concerted effort by a large section of the city that actually sees the writing on the wall that democratic machine power is detrimental."

"Education is at the crossroads of communities where people who live in the city send their children. If resources were allocated in the right way, it could shift the whole process in the way Philadelphia works [and] improve the living condition of folks on the ground in the city, but also improve the schools and the conditions of students in those schools, if we just change the role of education and the teachers unions in Philadelphia," he said. Jimenez said funding disparities exist, even when one controls for race—regardless of income level, majority-Black schools in Pennsylvania receive less per pupil funding than majority-White schools, he said.

"I think Philadelphia kind of exists in that unique parallel universe where we have a so-called liberal-running government in the city, but nothing has changed, in terms of how we sort of allocate resources, push for change and challenge the status quo. ... Their unwillingness to even engage in conversation is kind of a demonstration of that old power structure. As a consequence of this, a lot of students in our school are just shuffled along and kind of caught up in trying to maintain what already exists," rather than effect change, he said.

In 2017, a cadre of local educators launched Black Lives Matter at School National Week of Action, inspired by their counterparts in Seattle who'd dedicated a day to bringing issues of racial justice into the classroom. The aim was to both affirm students' identities and promote engagement and shed light on the critical issues facing students and teachers of color around the country. The movement's curriculum is centered around integrating culturally diverse opinions and discussions that encourage students to gain deeper understanding of pertinent issues affecting our students and their classmates. And demanding an increase in the hiring of Black teachers in the district, in 2018, the movement caught on in several other cities, and the National Education Association endorsed Black Lives Matter at School National Week of Action for the 2017–2018 school year, and has included it in the association's social justice platform.

The work doesn't end there. A group of educators in the city has also banded together to form The Fellowship: Black Male Educators for Social Justice, a network of men working to increase their representation in the profession; currently, only 2% of teachers in the U.S. are Black males, but the group hopes to recruit 1,000 Black men to Philadelphia's teaching force by 2025 and elevate that number to 11%.

Getting teachers of color into schools is not nearly as challenging as retaining them, said Jimenez. Black teachers who are seen as good at what they do are quickly taken out of the classroom and "pushed into disciplinarian roles," and many others "aren't viewed for their intellectual acuity as much as for tokenism," he said.

The combination of curriculum issues, staffing issues, resource issues, social issues and facility issues has agitated educators and others in the city into action. "Teaching in Black schools requires more than just teaching," Crawford said.

Jimenez said the Caucus modeled after efforts in Chicago and has tried to learn from the movement's early mistakes: in Chicago, he said, failing to address issues around race and racial justice created barriers to educators' efforts to organize. In Philly, "We don't look at race through a social justice lens, we look at social justice through a racial justice lens, and we realize that we can't move the needle on anything without addressing that elephant in the room of racial injustice that even our country hasn't done a good job with," he said.

But to avoid falling into the same pattern of maintaining the status quo and being victims of their own success, Jimenez believes strongly that the efforts must remain grassroots run, and must involve a clear articulation of goals; simply mobilizing to register voters and get people to show up at the polls is not enough, he said, noting "Philadelphia has the power to change the entire political landscape of our state."

There is work to be done, specifically around communicating the role of community members and how school governance actually operates, and to be more direct about individuals and families can be involved. Though the process for going into schools is dictated by state law, he said the school district and teachers union can work to streamline the process and encourage more people to volunteer in schools. And there needs to be more of a grassroots effort to dictate curriculum he said, "instead of relying on state standardized tests and private education technology companies to dictate where we're going." Smaller class sizes, retaining students and teachers of color and putting substantial money or services behind those efforts are among the goals that he has identified as needing real attention.

"Philadelphia is a city where people take great pride in where they went to school, so there's a lot of good investment in that," said Whack. "When you find a school where parents and the community are highly engaged, most often it's a good school. When you have a high level of engagement like that, it's not often that you see a school that's failing and doesn't have a high level of hope for the future."

REFERENCES

Bond, B., Quintero, E., Casey, L., & Di Carlo, M. (2015). *The State of Teacher Diversity in American Education*(Rep.). Retrieved http://www.shankerinstitute. org/resource/teacherdiversity

Graham, K. A. (2015, March 14). PA's spending gap widest in the nation. *Philadelphia Inquirer*. Retrieved from http://www.philly.com/philly/news/local/20150314_ Pa__s_school-spending_gap_widest_in_nation.html

Graham, K. A. (2017, June 19). Philly teachers OK new contract; now. how to pay for it? *Philadelphia Tribune*. Retrieved from http://www.philly.com/ philly/education/philly-teachers-ok-new-labor-contract-now-how-to-pay-for-it-20170620.html

Hanna, M. (2018, July 6). Gap between rich and poor Pa. school districts has grown, funding lawsuit says. *Philadelphia Inquirer*. Retrieved from http://www. philly.com/philly/education/pennsylvania-school-funding-lawsuit-rich-poor-districts-20180706.html

CONCLUSION

This investigation could have included any cities in America, and the themes likely would have been the same: Lower funding and resources, disproportionate numbers of teachers and school leaders who do not look like the students they serve, debates over the public's responsibility to provide fair and equitable education for all students in the jurisdiction, implicit biases from the top to the bottom and a resegregation of schools in America, as White families continue to strive to preserve Whiteness in their communities and their schools. Indeed, the entire 2016 election, which saw even educated and more liberal Whites voting for the bigoted Donald Trump, seems to have centered itself around the idea of preserving Whiteness above all else. (The irony, of course, is that the territories that would make up this nation were completely free of White bodies before individuals immigrated to this country seeking freedom from religious and social persecution and what they saw as expanded economic opportunities for themselves and their posterity.)

Integration for Black families was never about an idea that Black students were better off if they could be around White students, it was about the idea that Black students would be better off if they could have access to the same education that White students had—but residential segregation still enables de facto school segregation, when it isn't coded into policy.

In the schools that are more mixed, either through bussing or through families managing to break through discriminatory lending and real estate steering and zoning practices to integrate neighborhoods, you see clear

Let's Stop Calling It an Achievement Gap, pp. 117–121
Copyright © 2019 by Information Age Publishing

discrepancies in how discipline is applied to suspend students of color and keep them out of the classroom. There is persistent overpolicing of Black neighborhoods, as the institution is primarily leveraged to reinforce social norms and remind the people living there to stay in their places, thanks to both Richard Nixon's War on Drugs and Bill Clinton's crime bill (Guo, 2016). And the same overpolicing in schools, with more arrests for minor infractions compared to their White counterparts continue to plague Black students (Gordon, 2018).

But for the overwhelming majority of Black students, they're stuck in segregated, underperforming schools. Schools where the teachers are dedicated to the mission, but where the cities and districts and states have failed to uphold their basic responsibility to maintain the upkeep of the schools and provide enough desks for each child and current textbooks. Where, in places like Flint—or even Baltimore—the students can't even drink the water that comes out of the fountains. Where, even when they're able to get an influx of money from private donors and hope to add in something like a science lab to enhance the opportunities for the children in those schools, they have to apply that money to cover the failure of the system to provide schools in good condition. And states like Maryland continue to hide behind funding models that rely on local income taxes as an excuse why children in Baltimore City have grossly disparate educational experiences from those in the county that surround them—there isn't enough money coming in from local taxes to put more into the city schools, so they'll continue to be in disrepair, despite the fact that the state as a whole is the richest in the country, based on median household income (American's Richest (and Poorest) States, 2016).

Several of the cities in this investigation have been considered Ground Zero for education reform and, in particular, the school choice movement. Milwaukee, New Orleans and Chicago, in particular have been impacted by the influx of charter schools. The National Association for the Advancement of Colored People once called for a moratorium or charter schools, and many cite charter schools as being complicit in the resegregation of schools. However, charter schools themselves are not the enemy of Black students, and an argument which is simply pro- or anti-charter lacks the nuances of the total system of education as a failure to Black students.

Some charter systems come in with no local influence or connection to the communities or understanding of place—they bring in teachers and administrators who very often don't look like the students they're serving and have no understanding of the communities in which those students live. But others do the complete opposite: They make a point to hire Black leaders and teachers, they instill curricula and programming which affirms students' identities and promotes and increased sense of self. However, the lack of consistency and accountability and broad variation in standards from one school to the next is problematic, and can turn a movement heralded on the idea of giving families additional choices into something which actually limits those families' opportunities to guarantee their students a good education. If only a few of the new schools are actually schools families would desire—and everyone is vying for the same few—then it creates the same situation perpetuated by simply creating a few magnet programs in traditional community schools. And if funding is not equally distributed—charter schools must raise a majority of their operating funding privately—then there remain inequities between Black- and White-run charter schools, and create the same instability and frequent turnover when schools are forced to continuously bring in new authorizers. In essence, the system remains exactly the same as the one it sought to improve—and many public school administrators believe that if given the same room to innovate, select curriculum and govern their schools as they see fit as is afforded to charters, they would be able to make significant changes with the same population.

I do not foresee a circumstance in which the funding models in this country ever prioritize equity, but through conversations with stakeholders in each city contained within these chapters, the hope is there is something of a road map for individual districts and school leaders to begin to move forward to correct some of the adult-created, driven and maintained factors which make up the achievement gap.

RECOMMENDATIONS

1. Prioritize hiring teachers, administrators and staff who look like the students in the school, and whose backgrounds are similar to those of the students in the school. Implement something of a "Rooney Rule" for education: If you don't have applications from qualified individuals who meet the bill before you, go out and find them. Don't know where to start? Try approaching graduates of historically Black colleges and universities, many of which were founded as teachers colleges. Having people in the building who can relate to students is key to reducing the biases which perpetuate low expectations, and thus low achievement.

2. "De-colonize" the curriculum. As important as it is for students to see adults in the building who look like them, it is equally important for them to be given texts which affirm their identity and with which they can identify—and most importantly which do not contradict their senses of self. Black students, for instance, face cognitive dissonance when reading texts which dilute the atrocities of the

slave trade or call enslaved Africans "workers" or suggest African-Americans are descendants of "immigrants."

3. Invest the time and the effort to embrace and train staff in culturally relevant pedagogy and embrace the strengths students bring to the table, rather than focusing on deficits. Speaking a language other than English, including African American Vernacular English (ebonics) and being able to express one's self in multiple ways is not a negative trait. Understanding how students express themselves differently is directly related to discipline referrals and the increase in the number of citations for disrespectful behavior, as well as the interpretation that Black students are more dangerous than their White counterparts.

REFERENCES

America's Richest (And Poorest) States. (2016, September 15). Retrieved from https://www.huffingtonpost.com/entry/americas-richest-and-poorest-states_us_57db167be4b04fa361d99639

Gordon, N. (2018, January 18). Disproportionality in student discipline: Connecting policy to research. Retrieved https://www.brookings.edu/research/disproportionality-in-student-discipline-connecting-policy-to-research/

Guo, J. (2016, May 2). America's tough approach to policing Black communities began as a liberal idea. *The Washington Post*. Retrieved from https://www.washingtonpost.com/news/wonk/wp/2016/05/02/americas-tough-approach-to-policing-black-communities-began-as-a-liberal-idea/?noredirect=on&utm_term=.d462ae609819

ABOUT THE AUTHOR

Autumn A. Arnett is a Washington, D.C.-based journalist whose work focuses primarily on issues around diversity and access in K–12 and higher education, Black male achievement and the overall achievement gap, and issues surrounding student-athletes and the business of intercollegiate sports.